BASS RECORDED VERSIONS

ROCK BASS BIBLE

ROCK BASS BIBLE

ISBN 0-634-02216-4

HAL•LEONARD® CORPORATION

7777 W. Bluemound Rd. P.O. Box 13819 Milwaukee, WI 53213

Visit Hal Leonard Online at
www.halleonard.com

TABLE OF CONTENTS

Another One Bites the Dust

Words and Music by John Deacon

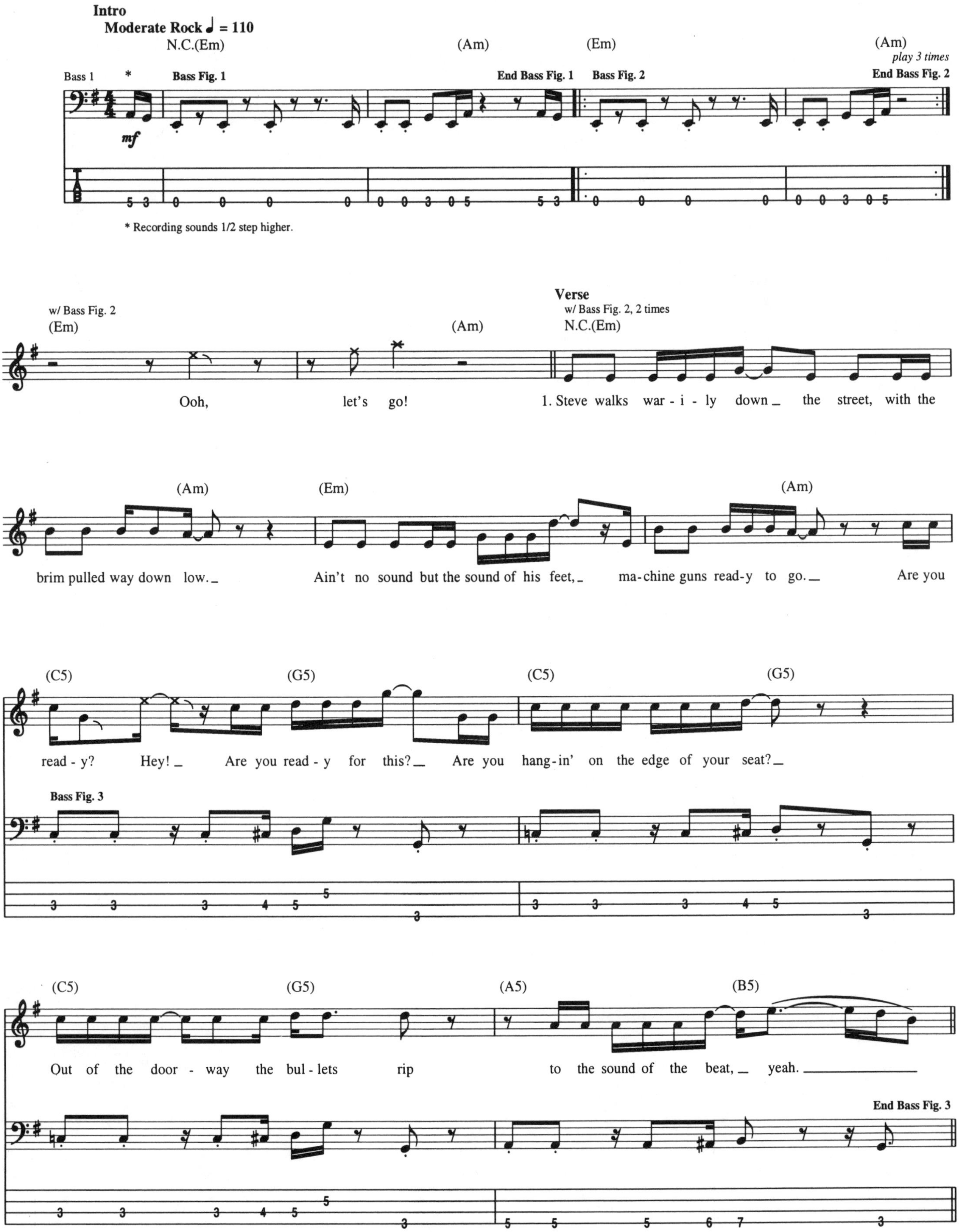

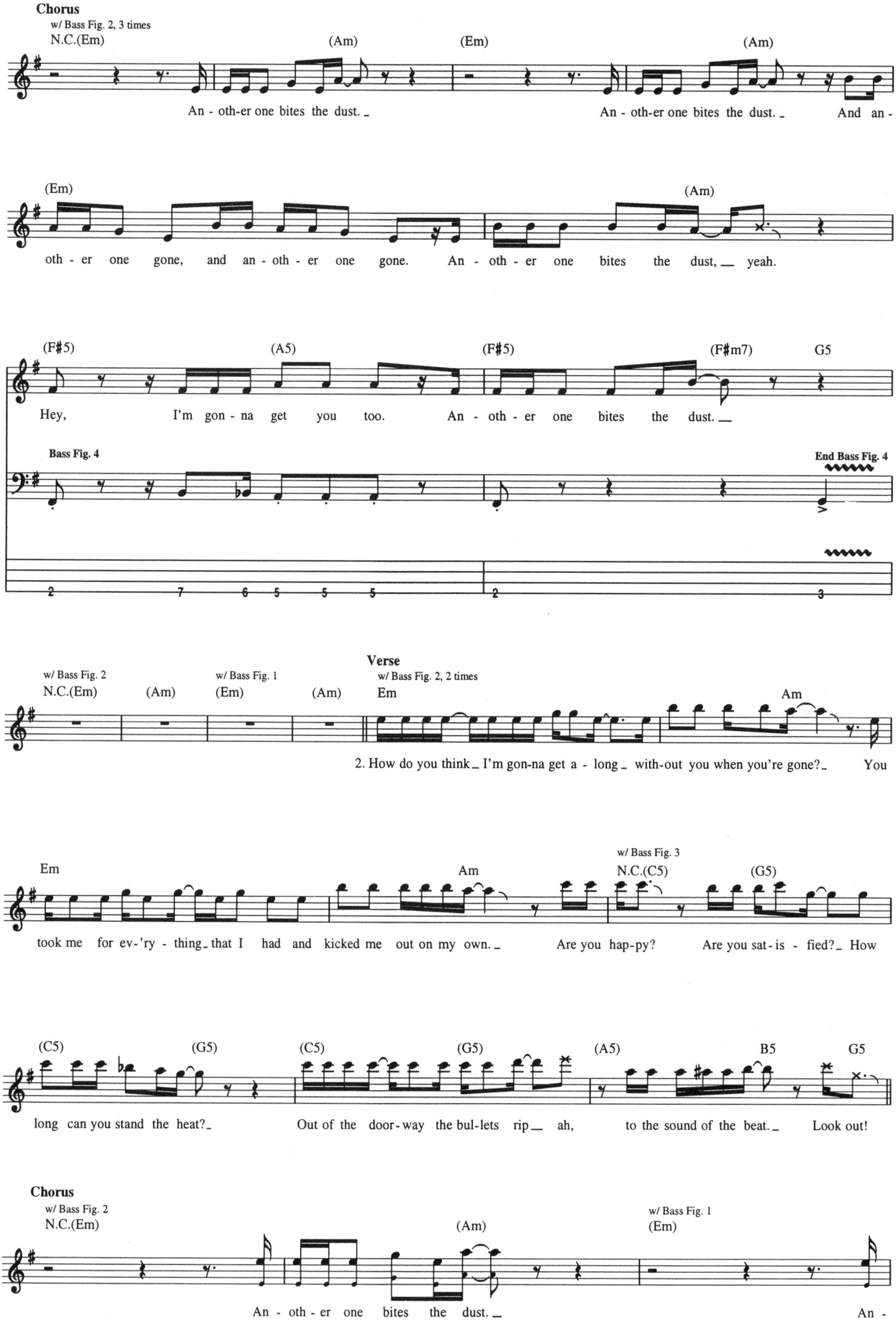
Chorus
w/ Bass Fig. 2, 3 times
N.C.(Em) (Am) (Em) (Am)
An - oth-er one bites the dust. An - oth-er one bites the dust. And an -
(Em) (Am)
oth - er one gone, and an - oth - er one gone. An - oth - er one bites the dust, yeah.
(F#5) (A5) (F#5) (F#m7) G5
Hey, I'm gon - na get you too. An - oth - er one bites the dust.
Bass Fig. 4
End Bass Fig. 4
2 7 6 5 5 5 2 3
Verse
w/ Bass Fig. 2
N.C.(Em) (Am)
w/ Bass Fig. 1
(Em) (Am)
w/ Bass Fig. 2, 2 times
Em Am
2. How do you think I'm gon-na get a - long with-out you when you're gone? You
Em Am
w/ Bass Fig. 3
N.C.(C5) (G5)
took me for ev-'ry - thing that I had and kicked me out on my own. Are you hap-py? Are you sat - is - fied? How
(C5) (G5) (C5) (G5) (A5) B5 G5
long can you stand the heat? Out of the door-way the bul-lets rip ah, to the sound of the beat. Look out!
Chorus
w/ Bass Fig. 2
N.C.(Em) (Am)
w/ Bass Fig. 1
(Em)
An - oth - er one bites the dust. An -

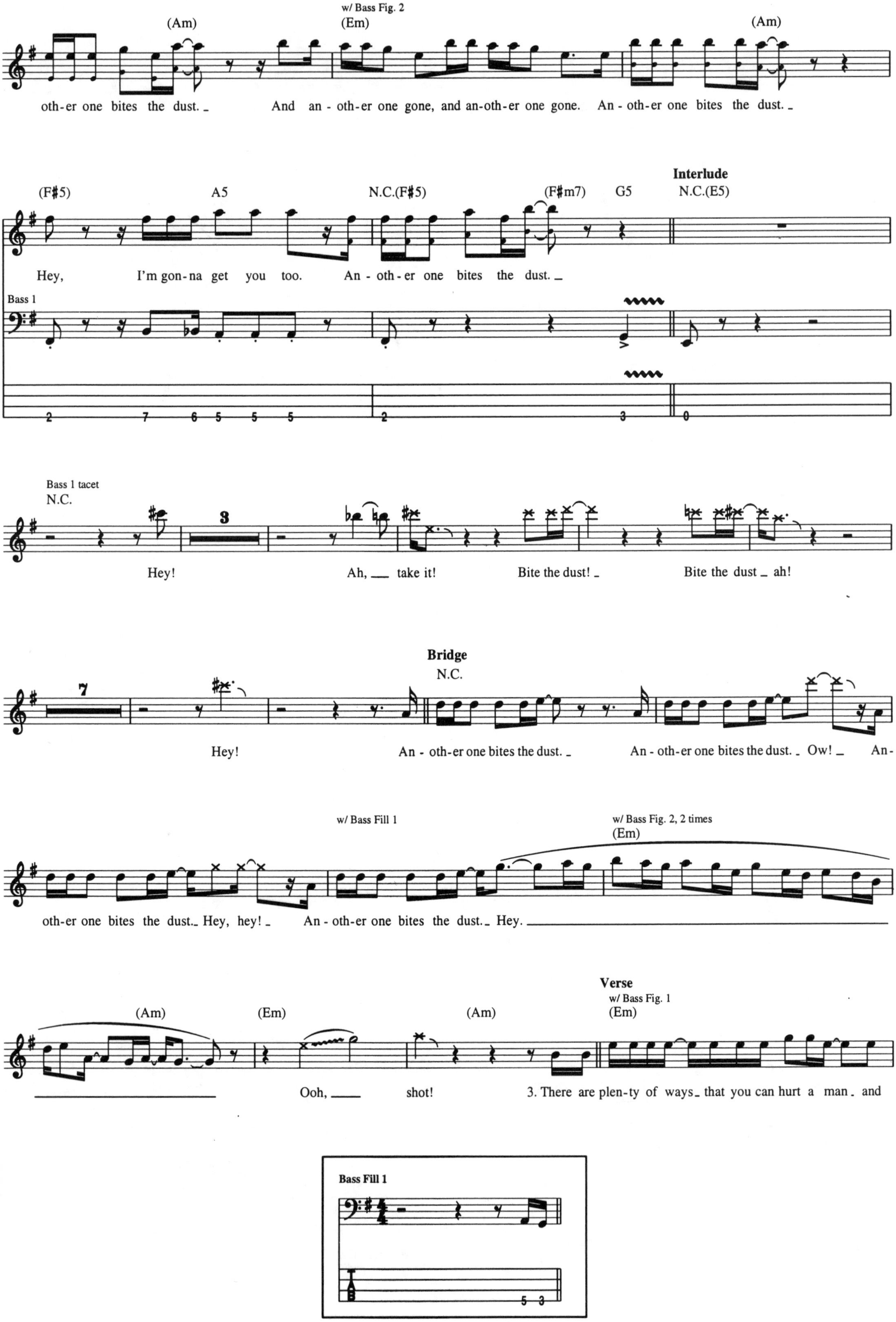
(Am)
w/ Bass Fig. 2
(Em)
(Am)
oth-er one bites the dust.
And an - oth-er one gone, and an-oth-er one gone. An - oth-er one bites the dust.
Interlude
(F♯5)
A5
N.C.(F♯5)
(F♯m7)
G5
N.C.(E5)
Hey, I'm gon-na get you too. An - oth-er one bites the dust.
Bass 1
2 7 6 5 5 5 2 3 0
Bass 1 tacet
N.C.
3
Hey!
Ah, take it!
Bite the dust!
Bite the dust ah!
Bridge
N.C.
7
Hey!
An - oth-er one bites the dust.
An - oth-er one bites the dust. Ow! An-
w/ Bass Fill 1
w/ Bass Fig. 2, 2 times
(Em)
oth-er one bites the dust. Hey, hey! An - oth-er one bites the dust. Hey.
Verse
w/ Bass Fig. 1
(Am)
(Em)
(Am)
(Em)
Ooh, shot!
3. There are plen-ty of ways that you can hurt a man and
Bass Fill 1
5 3

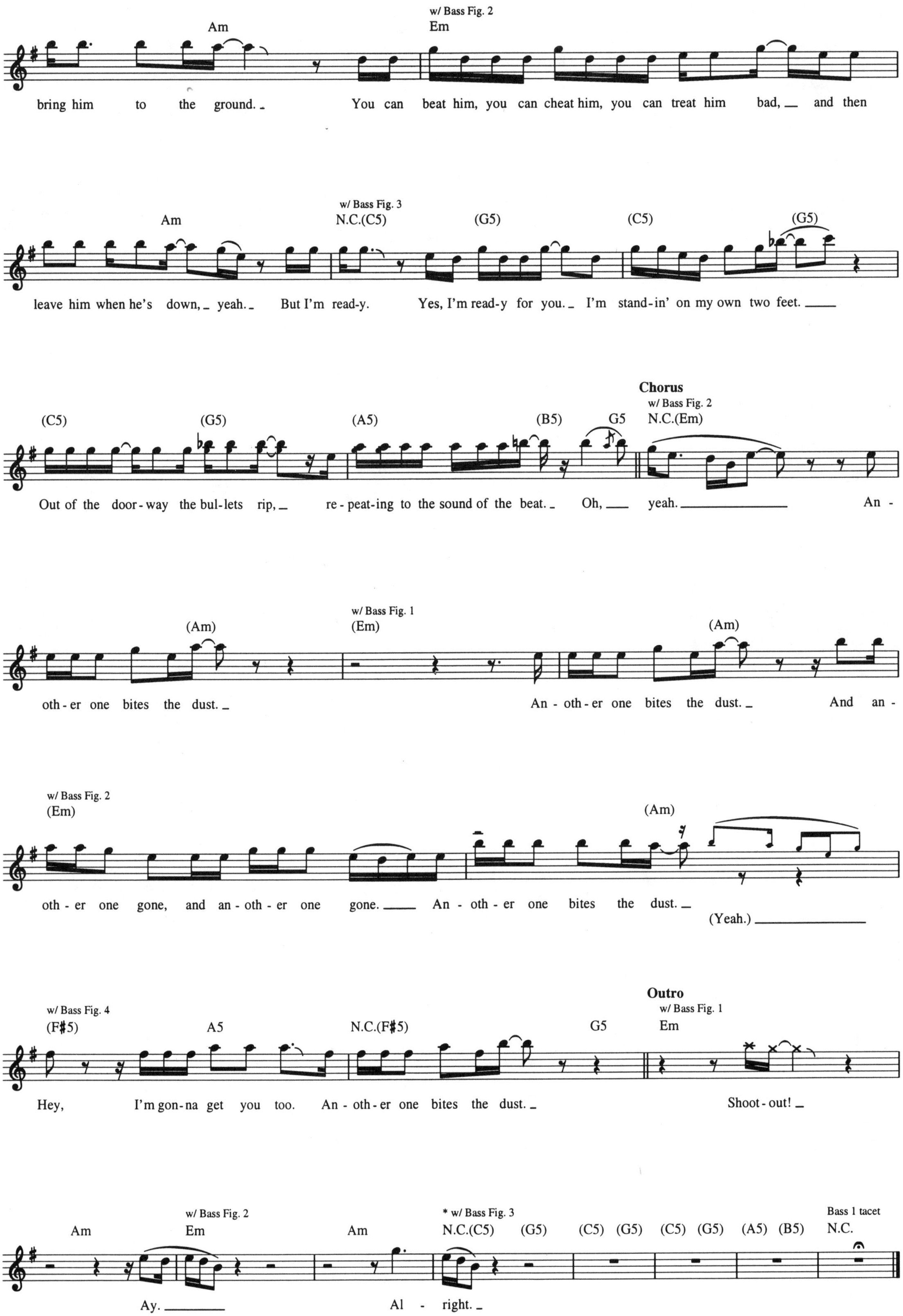

* Omit last note of Bass Fig. 3.

Badge

Words and Music by Eric Clapton and George Harrison

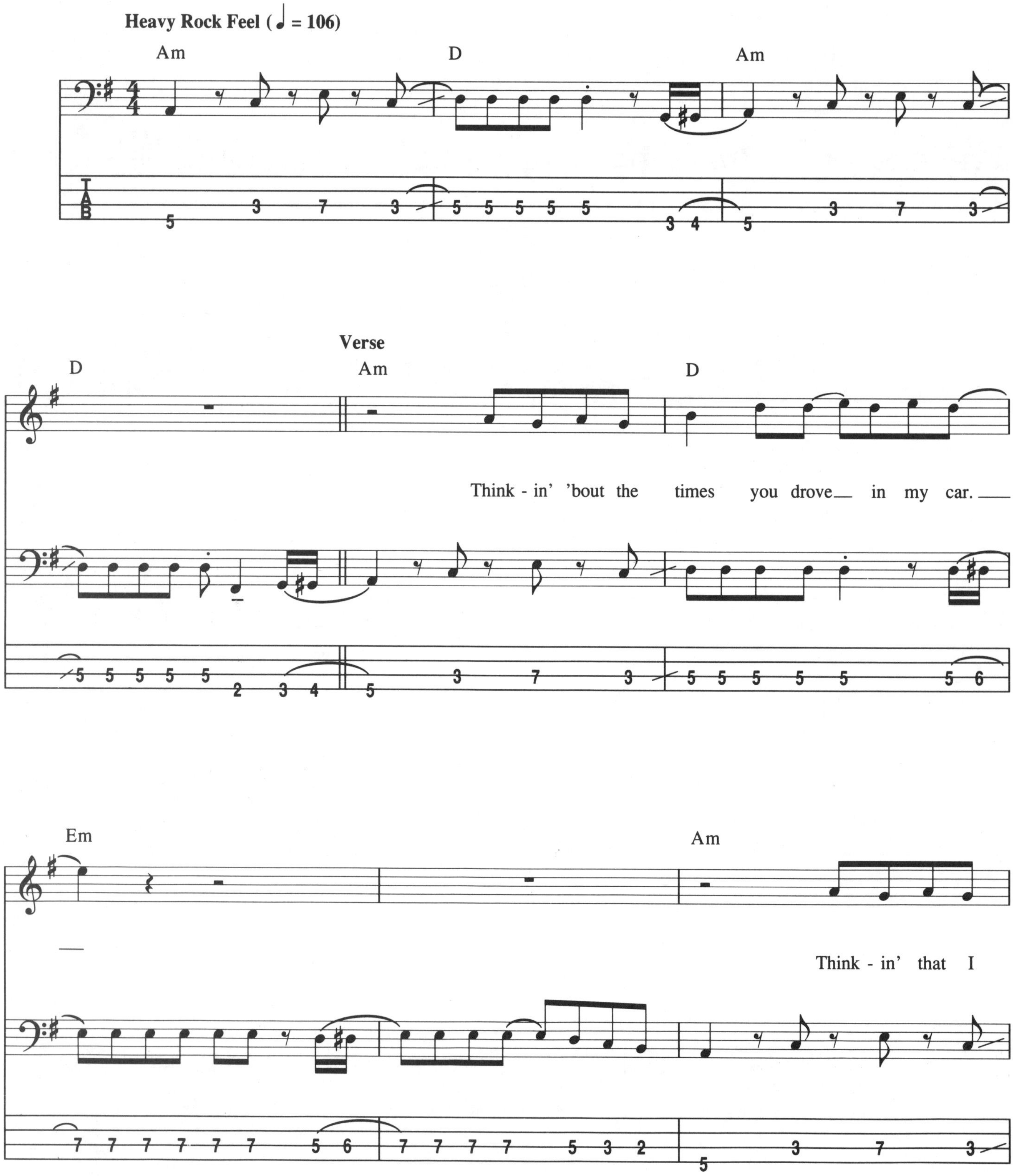

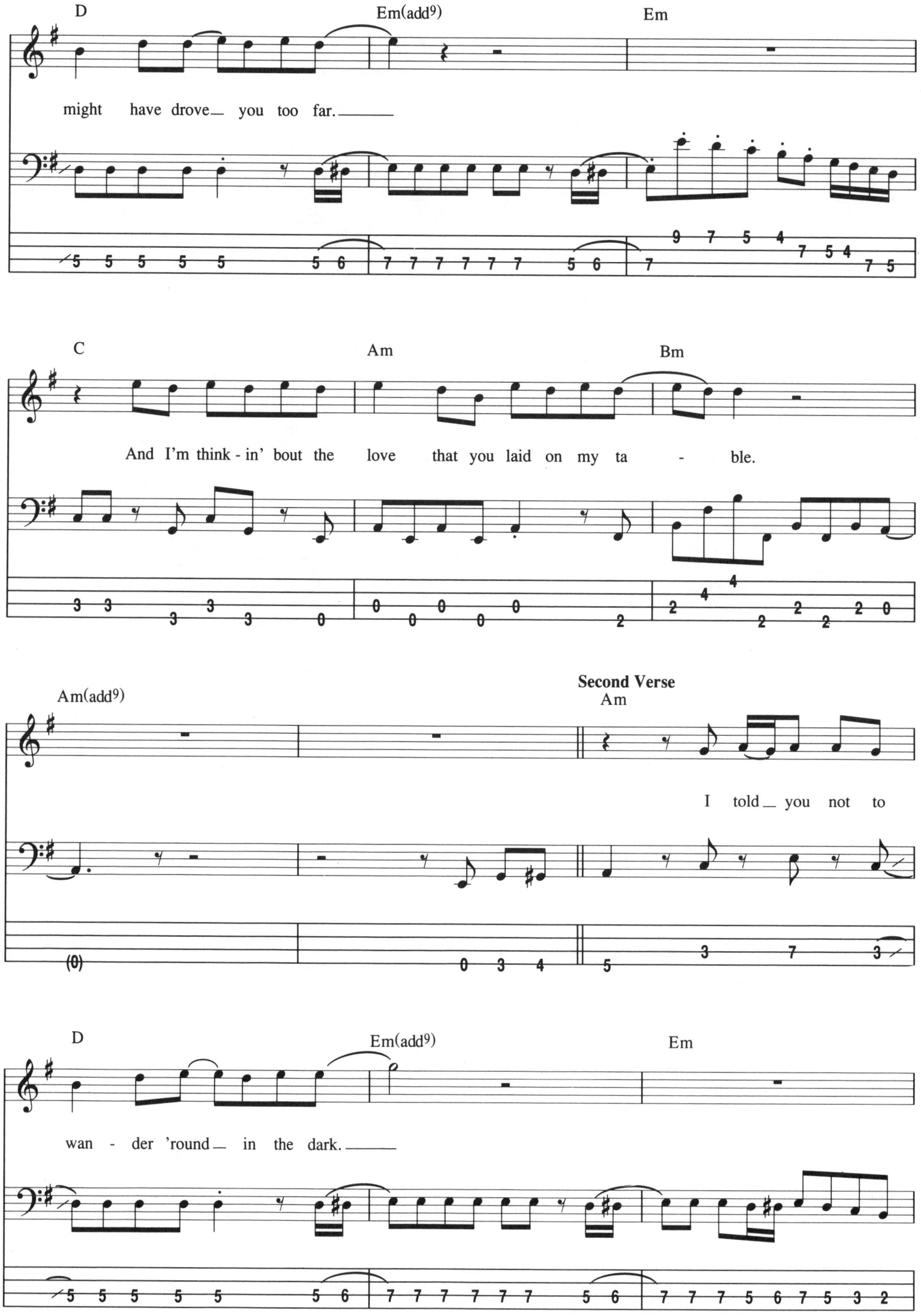
D
Em(add9)
Em
might have drove you too far.
C
Am
Bm
And I'm think - in' bout the love that you laid on my ta - ble.
Am(add9)
Second Verse
Am
I told you not to
D
Em(add9)
Em
wan - der 'round in the dark.

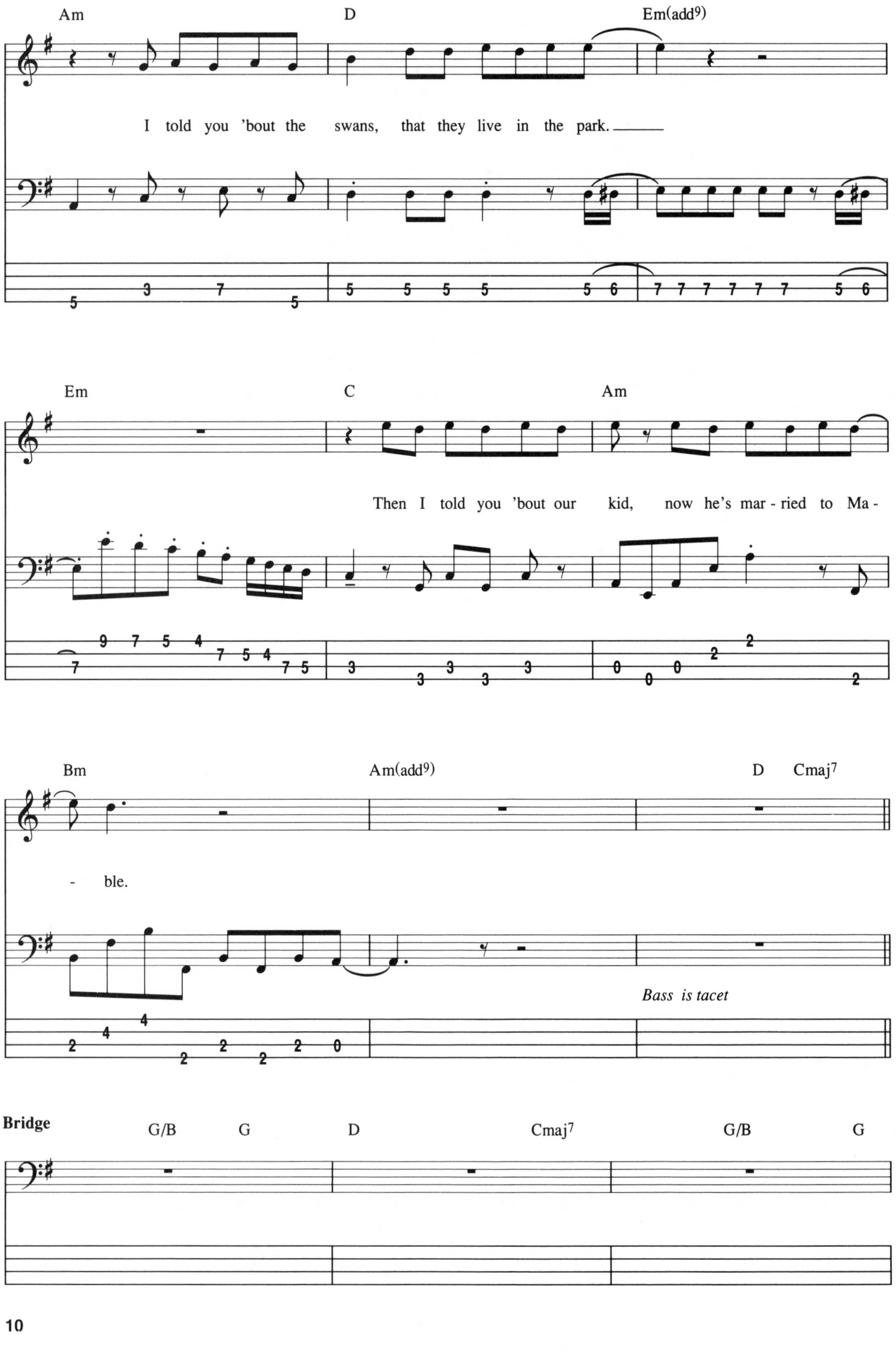
Am D Em(add9)
I told you 'bout the swans, that they live in the park.
Em C Am
Then I told you 'bout our kid, now he's mar - ried to Ma -
Bm Am(add9) D Cmaj7
- ble.
Bass is tacet
Bridge
G/B G D Cmaj7 G/B G

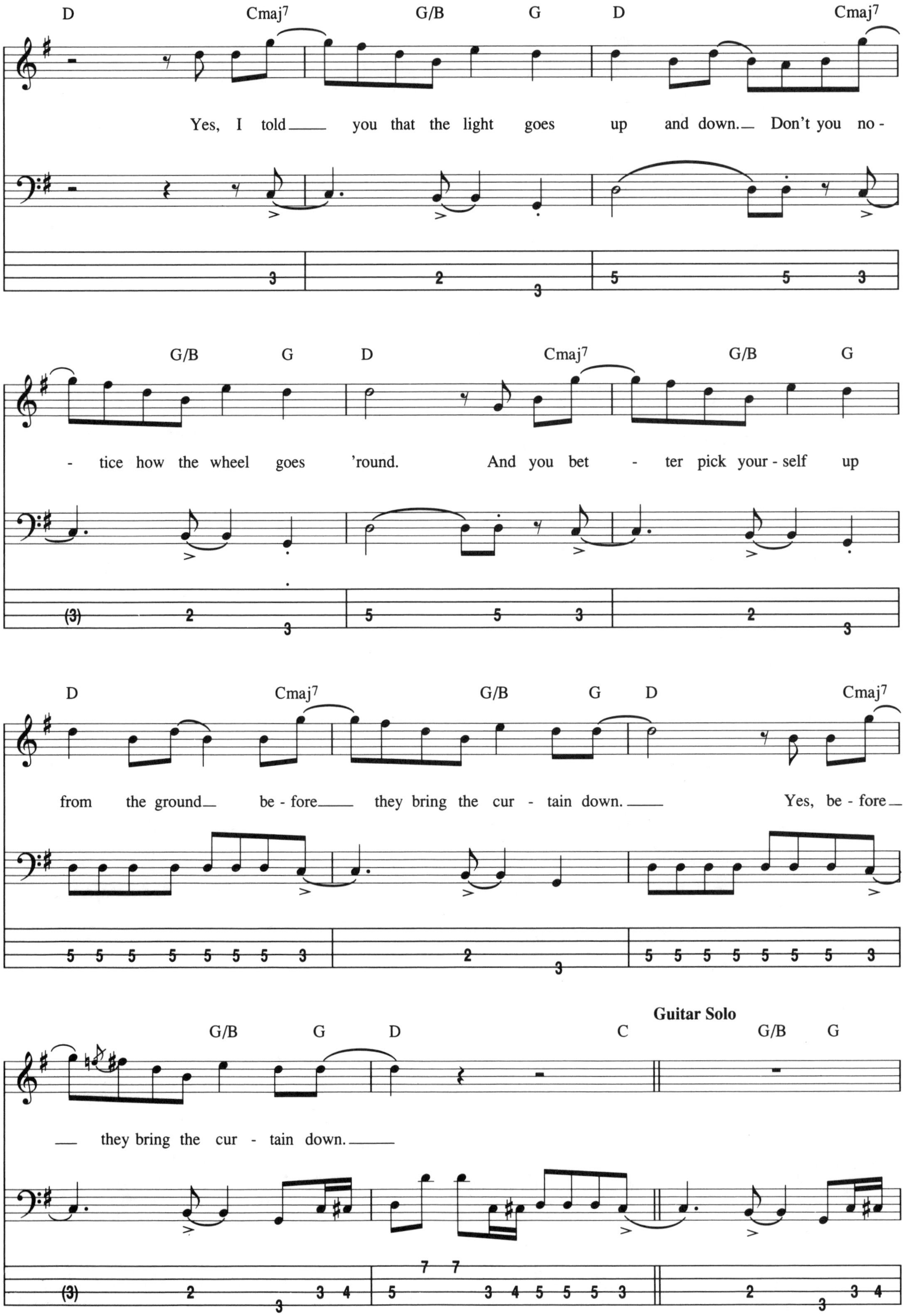
D Cmaj7 G/B G D Cmaj7
Yes, I told you that the light goes up and down. Don't you no-
G/B G D Cmaj7 G/B G
tice how the wheel goes 'round. And you bet - ter pick your-self up
D Cmaj7 G/B G D Cmaj7
from the ground be-fore they bring the cur - tain down. Yes, be-fore
G/B G D C G/B G
Guitar Solo
they bring the cur - tain down.

D
Cmaj7
G/B
G
D
Cmaj7
G/B
G
D
Cmaj7
G/B
G
D
Cmaj7
G/B
G
D
Cmaj7
G/B
G
D
Cmaj7
G/B
G
D
Cmaj7

Third Verse
D
Am
D
Talk - in' 'bout a girl that looks— quite like
Em(add9)
Am
you.
She did - n't have the
D
Em
time to wait— in the queue.
C
Am
Bm
Am(add9)
Fine
She cried a - way her life since she fell off the cra - dle.

Barracuda

Words and Music by Roger Fisher, Nancy Wilson, Ann Wilson and Michael Derosier

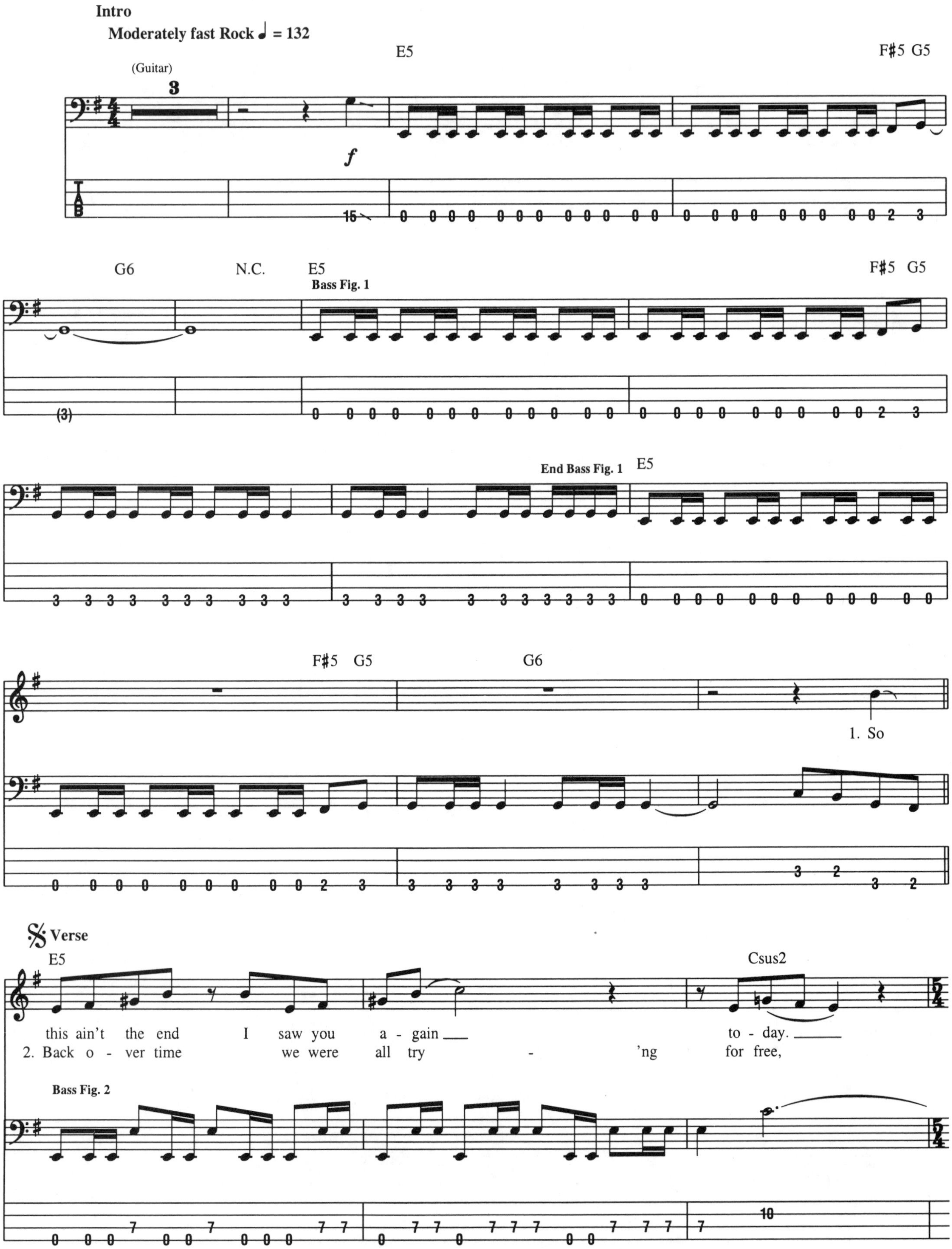

C5/B Am7 G5 E5
I had to turn my heart a - way.
you met the por-poise and me.
Uh huh.
End Rhy. Fig. 2
w/ Bass Fig. 2
E5
Csus2
Smile like the sun, kiss - es for ev - 'ry - one,
No right, no wrong; sell - ing a song, a name.
C5/B Am7 G5 E5
and tales that nev - er fail.
Whis - per game.
You ly - ing
And if the
Chorus
2nd time, w/ Bass Fill 1
To Coda
C5 C5/B N.C.(A5) E5 N.C.(C) (Am) E5
so low in - to the weeds. I bet you gon-na am - bush me. You'd have me
real thing don't do the trick, you bet-ter make up some-thing quick. You gon-na
Bass Fill 1

Dsus2
Asus2
down, down, down, down on my knees, now would-n't you, Bar - ra - cu -
w/ Bass Fig. 1
E5
F#5 G5
da? Oh.
E5
F#5 G5
G6
D.S. al Coda
Coda
Dsus2
Asus2
burn, burn, burn, burn, burn it to the wick.
E5
G5 A5 D5 E5
Ooh, Bar - ra - cu - da. Oh, yeah.
Bass Fig. 3

Bridge
G5 A5 D5 E5 C
"Sell me, sell
End Bass Fig. 3
Bass Fig. 4
A
you," the por - poise said. Dive down, deep down, save my head. You,
End Bass Fig. 4
w/ Bass Fig. 3
E5
G5 A5 D5 E5
G5 A5 D5 E5 C
w/ Bass Fig. 4
I think that you had the blues too.
All that night
A
and all the next, swam with - out look - ing back, made for the west - ern
E5
F#5 G5 A5 E5
F#5 G5 A5
pools. Sil-ly, sil-ly fools.

Guitar Solo
C
A
E5
F#5 G5 A5
E5
1.
F#5 G5 A5
2.
F#5 G5 A5
Chorus
C5 C5/B N.C.(A5) E5
The real thing don't do the trick, no, you bet - ter
N.C.(C) (Am) E5 Dsus2
make up some - thing quick. You gon - na burn, burn, burn,

Asus2
burn, burn it to the wick.
(12) 14 12 11 14 12 11 14
12
12
E5
Oh, Bar - ra - bar -
ra - cu - da.
Yeah.
Outro
N.C.(Em)
Play 3 times

1.
2.
E5
1.-4.
F#5 G5 A5
5.
F#5 G5 A5

Carry on Wayward Son

Words and Music by Kerry Livgren

(♩. = ♩)
F#m7 Em7
Am
G Am G Fmaj7
Ah.
Verse
Bass tacet
Am G6 Fmaj7 G6 Am G6
1. Once I rose a - bove the noise and con - fu - sion, just to get a glimpse be -
Fmaj7 G6 Dm C B♭ C Dm C
yond this il - lu - sion. I was soar - ing ev - er high - er, but I flew too
G Am G6 Fmaj7 G6 Am G6
high. 'Though my eyes could see, I still was a blind man. 'Though my mind could think, I
mf
Fmaj7 G6 Dm C B♭ C Dm C
still was a mad - man. I hear the voi - ces when I'm dream - ing, I can hear them

Chorus
G Am C G Fsus2 Am C G
say: "Car-ry on my way - ward son. There'll be peace when you
Am C G Fadd9 F N.C.
are done. Lay your wear-y head to rest. Don't you cry no
w/ Bass Fig. 1 (2 times)
N.C. C D G D/F# C D G D/F#
more."
Verse
Am G6 Fmaj7 G6 Am G6
2. Mas-quer-ad-ing as a man with a rea - son. My cha-rade is the e -

Fmaj7 G6 Dm C Bb C
vent of the sea - son. And if I claim to be a wise man, ah,
Dm C G Am G6
it sure - ly means that I don't know. On a storm - y sea of
Fmaj7 G6 Am G6 Fmaj7 G6
mov - ing e - mo - tion. Tossed a - bout, I'm like a ship on the o - cean.
Dm C Bb C Dm C G
I set a course for winds of for - tune. But I hear the voi - ces say:

Chorus
2nd time, w/ Bass Fill 1
Am C G Fsus2 Am C G
"Car-ry on my way - ward son. There'll be peace when you are done.
Am C G Fadd9 F N.C.
To Coda
Lay your wear-y head to rest. Don't you cry no more, No!
Interlude
N.C.(Am) D5 C5 N.C.(Am) D5
N.C.(Am) D5 C5 N.C.(Am) D5
Bass Fill 1

Organ, Guitar Solo
N.C.
Interlude
N.C. C D G D/F#
Bridge
A5 N.C. G5 F5 N.C. A5 N.C. G5
Car - ry on, you will al - ways re - mem - ber.
Car - ry on, noth - ing
F5 N.C. D5 C5 B♭5 N.C.
e - quals the splen - dor.
Now your life's no long - er emp - ty,
D.S. al Coda
Coda
D5 C5 G5
Sure-ly, heav-en waits for you.
F N.C.
Don't you cry no
(Don't you cry.

(𝅗𝅥 = 𝅗𝅥.)
w/ Bass Fig. 2 (2 times)
E7#9
F#m7 Em7
more.
Em#9
F#m7 Em7
Guitar Solo
N.C.(F#m7)
A5
E5 N.C.(F#m7)
Play 3 times
A
E7/#9
F#m7 Em7
No more!
w/ Bass Fig. 2
E7♭9
F#m7 Em7
N.C.(F#m7)
A5
E5
Play 4 times
Am
G Am G
Fmaj7

Come Together

Words and Music by John Lennon and Paul McCartney

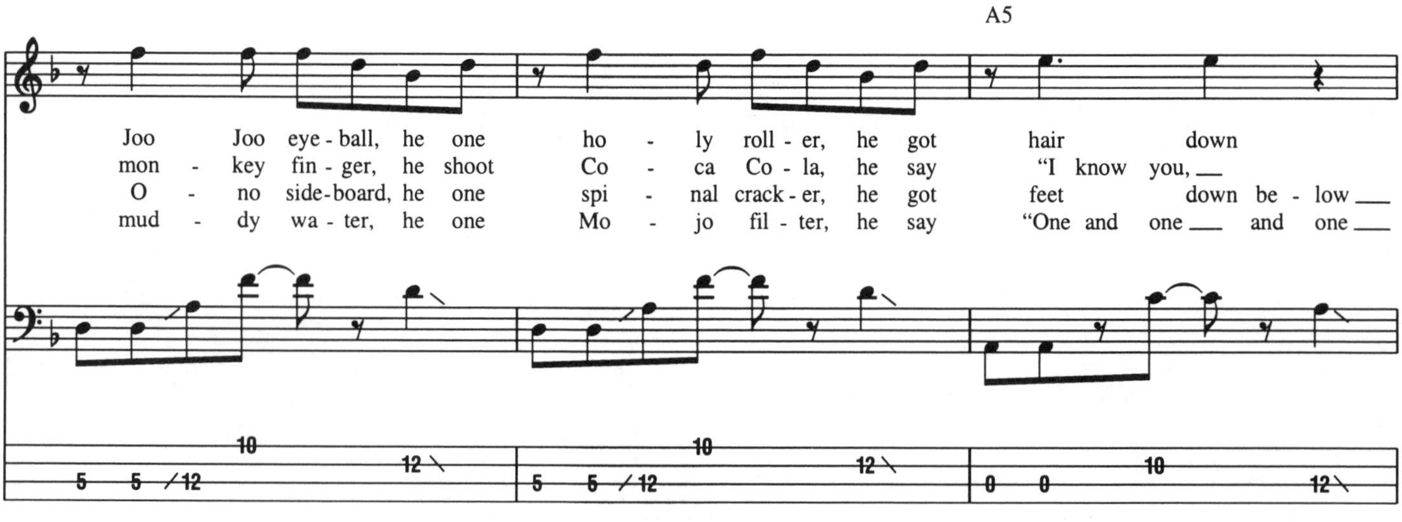

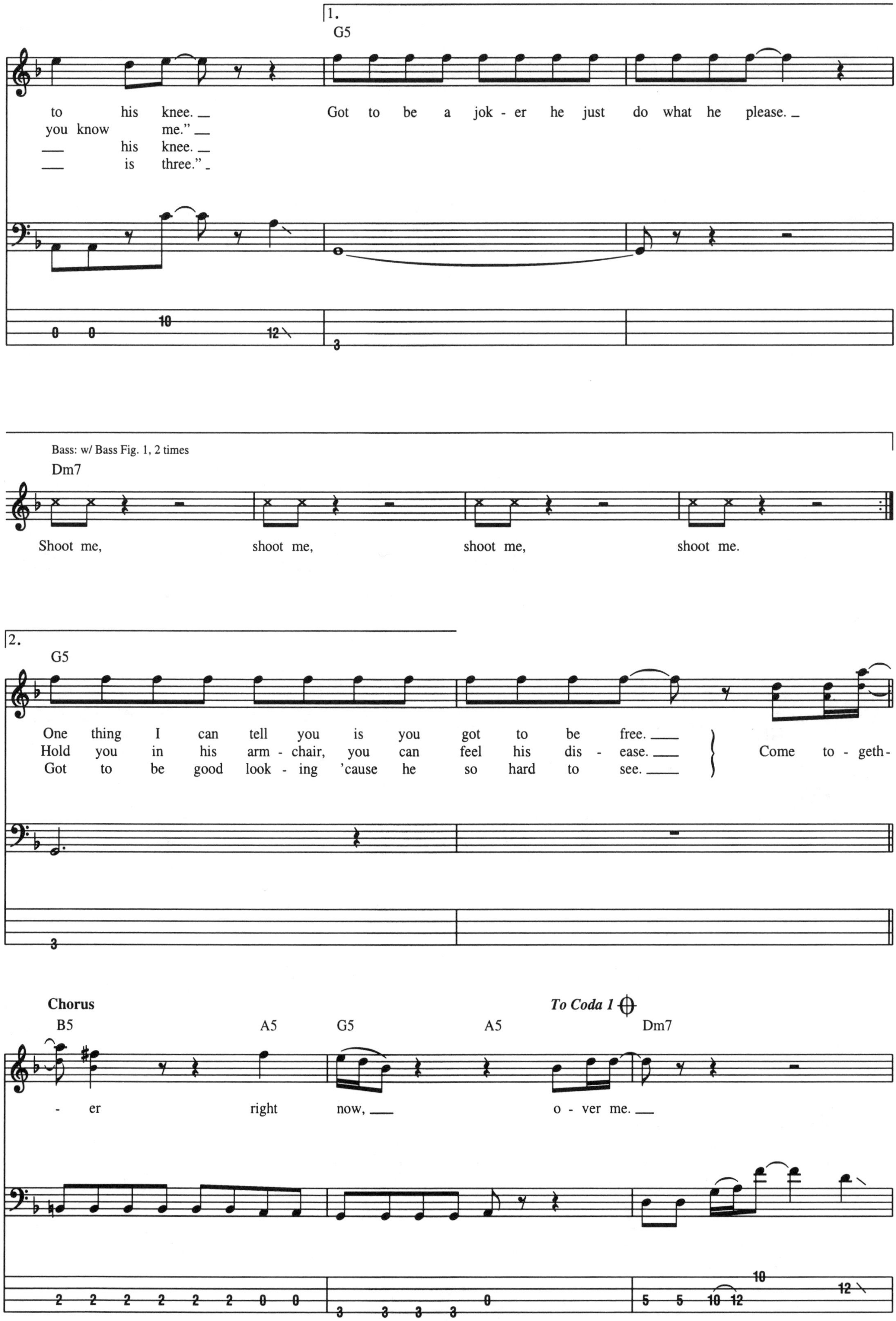
1.
G5
to his knee. Got to be a jok - er he just do what he please.
you know me."
his knee.
is three."
Bass: w/ Bass Fig. 1, 2 times
Dm7
Shoot me, shoot me, shoot me, shoot me.
2.
G5
One thing I can tell you is you got to be free.
Hold you in his arm - chair, you can feel his dis - ease.
Got to be good look - ing 'cause he so hard to see.
Come to - geth -
Chorus
To Coda 1
B5 A5 G5 A5 Dm7
- er right now, o - ver me.

To Coda 2
D.S. al Coda 1
(take 2nd ending)
Shoot me,
shoot me,
shoot me.
Coda 1
Dm7
Keyboard Solo
D5
Shoot me.
Right.
Come.

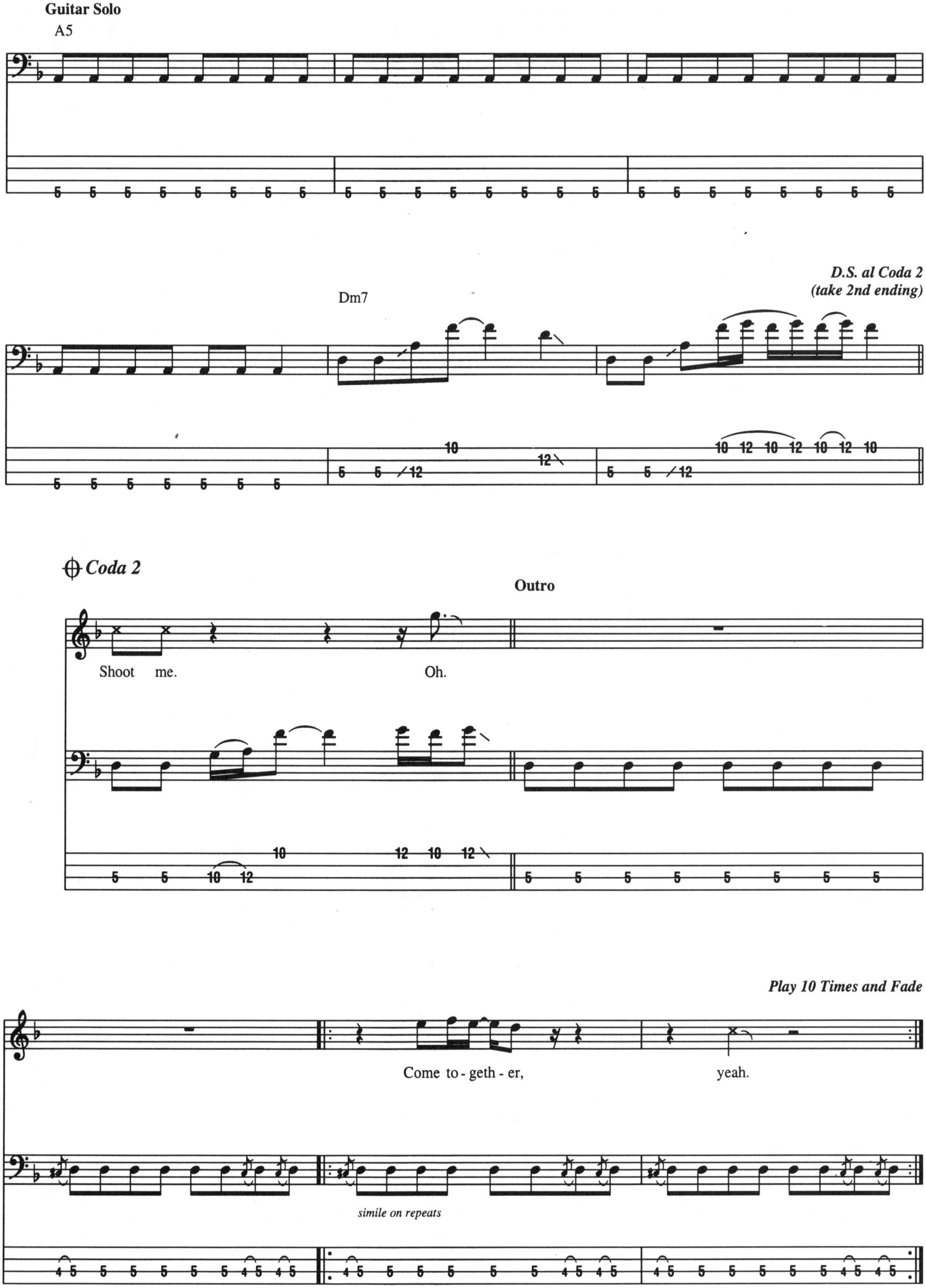
Guitar Solo
A5
D.S. al Coda 2
(take 2nd ending)
Dm7
Coda 2
Outro
Shoot me.
Oh.
Play 10 Times and Fade
Come to - geth - er,
yeah.
simile on repeats

Crossfire

Written by Bill Carter, Ruth Ellsworth, Reese Wynans, Tommy Shannon and Chris Layton

Tune Down 1/2 Step

①=G♭ ②=D♭

③=A♭ ④=E♭

Moderate "Bluesy" Rock ♩ = 112

A Introduction

Play 3 times

B Verse (E)
N.C.

C Chorus
(E♯7♯9)
N.C.
– ed, caught in the cross – fire.
Strand-ed, caught in the cross-fire.
D Verse
(E)
N.C.
2. Tooth for tooth, eye for an eye, sell your soul just to buy, buy, buy.
Beg-gin' a dol-lar, steal-in' a dime, come on can't cha see that I, I'm strand-

E Chorus
(E7#9)
N.C.
– ed? Caught in the cross - fire. I am strand-
– ed, caught in the cross – fire.
F Bridge
G A G A
I need some kind of kind-ness, some kind of sym-pa-thy, Oh no, we're
G Chorus
strand-ed, caught in the cross – fire.

H **Guitar Solo**

I **Verse**

Trust no-bod-y, don't be no fool._ What-ev-er hap-pened to the gold– en rule? We got strand-

J Chorus
(E7#9)
N.C.
– ed, caught in the cross - fire. We got strand –

– ed, caught in the cross – fire. We got strand-

K Chorus

- ed, ____ caught in the cross – fire.

Strand - ed, ____ caught in __ the cross - fire.
Help me!

L Guitar Solo

(E7)
N.C.
Play 7 times

Detroit Rock City

Words and Music by Paul Stanley and Bob Ezrin

Tune Down 1/2 Step:
① = G♭ ③ = A♭
② = D♭ ④ = E♭

Intro

Fast Rock ♩ = 184 Triplet Feel

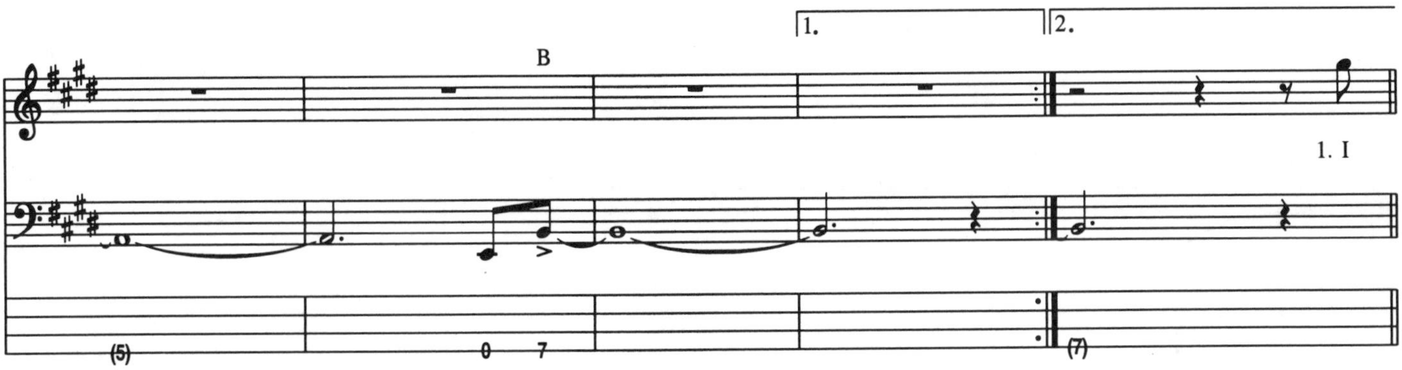

Verse

* Chord symbols derived from gtr.

E5
hear my song and it pulls me through.
B
F♯
A5
Comes on strong; tells me what I got - ta do.
I got to...
Get up!
Chorus
A5
B
Ev - 'ry-bod-y's gon-na move their feet. Get down! Ev - 'ry-bod-y's gon-na leave their seat.
N.C.(C♯m)
A
You got-ta lose your mind in De - troit Rock Cit - y. Get up!
B
Ev - 'ry-bod-y's gon-na move their feet. Get down! Ev - 'ry-bod-y's gon-na leave their seat.

Verse
C#5
E5
2. Get-ting late, _ I just can't wait.
B
F#
C#
Ten o' - clock, _ and I know I got-ta hit the road. ___
E5
First I drink, then I smoke.
B
F#
A5
Start the car, _ and I try to make the mid-night show. ___ Get up! _
Chorus
A5
B
_ Ev-'ry-bod-y's gon-na move their feet. Get down! _ Ev-'ry-bod-y's gon-na leave their seat. ___

Interlude
N.C.(C#m)
1.
2.
D#5
C#5
F#
E5
A5
B
Verse
C#5
E5
3. Mov-in' fast, do-in' nine - ty - five.
4. Twelve o'-clock, I got - ta rock.
There's a
B
F#
C#
Hit top speed, but I'm still mov-in' much too slow.
truck a - head, lights star-in' at my eyes.
I

E5
feel so good, I'm so a - live.
Oh my God! No time to turn.
I
To Coda
B
F#
A5
Hear my song play - in' on the ra - di - o. It goes:
got to laugh 'cause I know I'm gon-na die! Why?
Get up!
Chorus
A5
B
C#
Ev - 'ry-bod-y's gon-na move their feet. Get down! Ev - 'ry-bod-y's gon-na leave their seat.
Interlude
N.C.
(drums)
A5
B

N.C.(C#m)
D.S. al Coda
A5
B
Coda
A5
B
C#5
Ev - 'ry - bod - y's gon - na move their feet.
(drums)
A5
B
Get up! Ev - 'ry - bod - y's gon - na leave their seat.
w/ auto crash, explosion & gtr. siren effects
C#5

Drive My Car

Words and Music by John Lennon and Paul McCartney

Chorus
Bm
G
in be - tween."
bet - ter time."
that's a start."
"Ba - by, you can drive my car.
Bass Fig. 1
Bm
G
Bm
Yes, I'm gon - na be a star.
Ba - by, you can drive my car,
1.
To Coda
E
A
D
G
A
and may - be I'll love you."
End Bass Fig. 1
2.
D
G
A
N.C.
Guitar Solo
D
you."
Beep, beep, mm, beep, beep, yeah!
* Sing 1st time

G
A7#5#9
Play 3 times
Chorus
w/ Bass Fig. 1
Bm G Bm G
"Ba-by, you can drive my car.
Yes, I'm gon-na be a star.
D.S. al Coda
Bm E A D G A
Ba-by, you can drive my car, and may-be I'll love you."
Coda
Outro
D G A N.C. D G
you."
Beep, beep, mm, beep, beep, yeah!
Repeat and fade
A N.C. D G A N.C.
Beep, beep, mm, beep, beep, yeah!
Beep, beep, mm, beep, beep, yeah!

Fat Bottomed Girls

Words and Music by Brian May

D Csus2 A D D5
ev - ry blue-eyed floo - zy on the way. Hey. But their beau - ty and their style went kind of smooth
F5 G F5 D5 D Csus2 A D5
af - ter a while, take me to them dir - ty la - dies ev - 'ry - time. Shout!
End Bass Fig. 1
Chorus
D5 D C5 G/B D5 D G C5 G/B A
Oh, won't you take me home to-night? Oh, down be - side your red fire light.
Bass Fig. 2
D5 D G F5 G5 G D5 A5 D5
Oh, and you give it all you've got, fat bot-tomed girls, you make the rock-in' world go
End Bass Fig. 2

D G5 F5 D5 A5 D5 D G5 G/B D
'round. Fat bot-tomed girls, you make the rock-in' world go 'round.
1/4
A D G/B D A G5
Hey, lis-ten here, ah. 3. Now, I got
Verse
w/ Bass Fig. 1, simile
D G5 F5 D5 D Csus2
mort-ga-ges and homes, I got stiff-ness in my bones, ain't no beau-ty queens in this lo-cal-i-ty.
A D D5 F5 G F5 D5
I tell ya. Oh, but I still get my pleas-ure, still got my great-est treas-ure, heap big
D Csus2 A D5 G5
wom-an, you gon-na make a big man of me. Now get this.
Chorus
w/ Bass Fig. 2, simile
D5 D C5 G/B D5 D G
Oh, I know. Please. Oh, down be-side.
Oh, you gon-na take me home to-night?

C5 G/B A D5 D G F5 G5 G D5
that red fire - light. Oh, you got - ta let it all hang out, fat bot-tomed girls,
A5 D5 G D A5 D5
you make the rock-in' world go 'round. Fat bot-tomed girls, you make the rock-in' world go 'round.
Bass 1
1/4
Outro
D
Get on your bikes an' ride. Oo, yeah, uh. Oh, yeah.
Csus2 D
Them fat bot-tomed girls, they get me. Yeah, yeah, yeah.
(Fat bot-tomed girls.)

Al - right, ride 'em cow-boy.
Woo!
(Fat bot-tomed girls.)
Yes yes!
1/4

Hair of the Dog

Words and Music by Dan McCafferty, Darrell Sweet, Pete Agnew and Manuel Charlton

Intro

Moderate Rock ♩ = 128

** E7
(Drums)
Bass Fig. 1
End Bass Fig. 1
f
1/4
1/4

* Key signature denotes E Mixolydian.

** Chord symbols reflect implied harmony.

Verse

w/ Bass Fig. 1
E7
1. Heart break - er, soul shak - er, I've been told a - bout you.
2. Talk-in' jiv - ey, poi - son i - vy, you ain't gon-na cling to me.

Steam - roll - er, mid-night stroll - er, what they've been say - in' must be true.
Man tak - er, born fak - er, I ain't so blind I can't
1/4

A7
see.
Red hot ma - ma, vel - vet charm - er,
1/4
1/4

E7
time's come to pay your dues.
1/4
Chorus
E5
G5
Now you're mess-in' with a...
1/4
1/4
A5
E5
D5
E5
Now you're mess - in' with a son of a bitch.
Voc. Fig. 1
End Voc. Fig. 1
(A son of a bitch.)

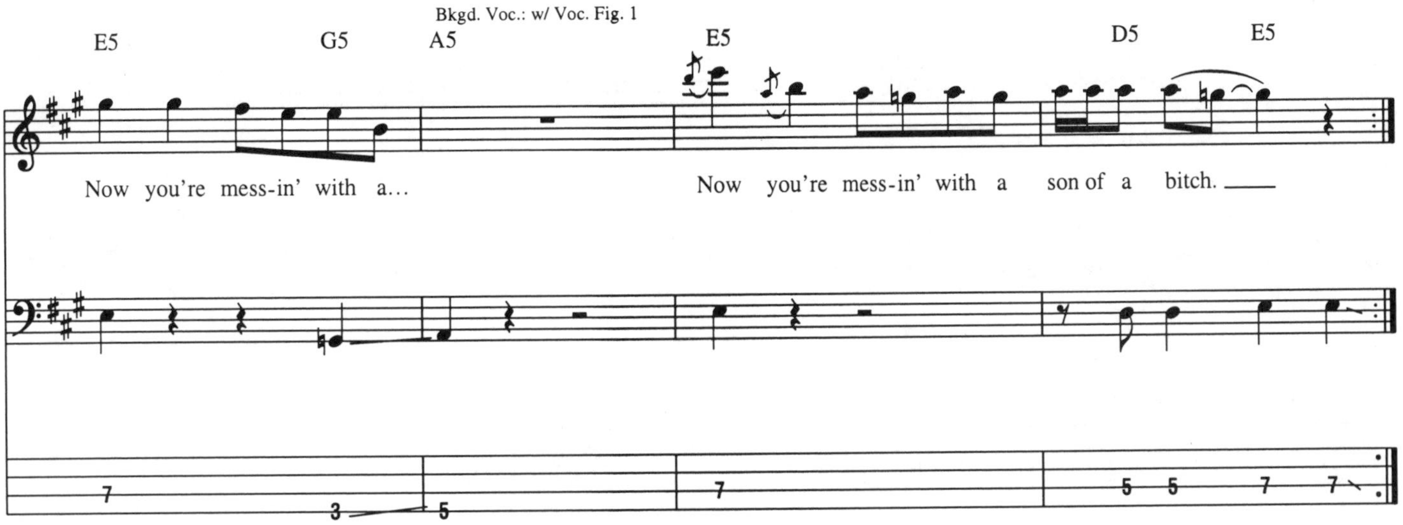
Bkgd. Voc.: w/ Voc. Fig. 1
E5
G5
A5
E5
D5
E5
Now you're mess-in' with a...
Now you're mess-in' with a son of a bitch.

Interlude

E7
1/4
1/4

E5
3
E5
G5
A5

E5
G5
A5
E5

1.
2.
D5
C5
B5
D5
C5
B5
E7
1/4

Chorus
Bkgd. Voc.: w/ Voc. Fig. 1
E5 G5/E A5/E
Now you're mess-in' with a...
1/4
E5 D5/E E5 G5/E
Now you're mess-in' with a son of a bitch.
Now you're mess-in' with a...
Bass Fig. 2
Bkgd. Voc.: w/ Voc. Fig. 1
A5/E E5 D5/E E5
Now you're mess-in' with a son of a bitch.
End Bass Fig. 2
Outro
w/ Bass Fig. 2 (till end)
Bkgd. Voc.:w/ Voc. Fig. 1
E5 G5 A5 E5 D5 E5
Now you're mess-in' with a...
Now you're mess-in' with a son of a bitch.
(Spoken: Son of a bitch.)
Bkgd. Voc.: w/ Voc. Fig. 1
Play 4 times and fade
E5 G5 A5 E5 D5 E5
Now you're mess-in' with a...
Now you're mess-in' with a son of a bitch.

Hey Joe

Words and Music by Billy Roberts

D Aadd9 E
you know I caught her mess-in' 'round with an-oth-er man.
Yeah!
C Gadd9
I'm go-in' down to shoot my old la-dy,
Ooh.
D A E
you know I caught her mess-in' 'round with an-oth-er man.
Huh! And that ain't
Verse
C G D A
too cool.
2. Uh, hey, Joe, I heard you shot your
(Ah.

E
C
G
wom-an down,_you shot her down, now. _
Uh, hey, _ Joe,
Ah.
D5
Aadd9
E
I heard you shot your old la - dy down, _ you shot her down in the ground. _
C
Gadd9
Yeah! _
Yes I _ did, I shot her,
Ah.
D5
A
E
you know I caught her mess-in' 'round, mess-in' 'round town. _

C Gadd9 D A
Uh, yes I did, I shot her, you know I caught my old la - dy mess-in' 'round
Ah.
E E7
town. And I gave her the gun, I shot her!
)
Guitar Solo
C Gadd9 D A E N.C.
Woo! Ah! Hey, Joe! Al - right!
E E7 C Gadd9 Dsus4 A N.C.
Shoot her one more time a - gain, ba-by! Ooh. Hey,

E7
Interlude
N.C.(C)
(G)
Yeah!
Ah, dig it!
Ah!
Joe!)
(Hey,
(D)
(A)
E
Ah!
Joe, where you gon - na go?)
Ooh, al - right!
Verse
C
G
D
A
E7
3. Hey, Joe, said now, uh, where you gon-na run to now, where you gon-na run to?
(Hey, Joe, where you gon - na go?
C
Gadd9
D
A
Yeah.
Hey, Joe, I said, where you gon-na run
Hey,

E
N.C.
C
Gadd9
_ to now, _ where you, where you gon-na go?
Well, dig it!
I'm go-in' way down south, _
Joe!
Hey,
D
A
E
N.C.
way down to Mex - i - co way!
Joe!
E
N.C.(C)
(G)
(D)
(A)
Al - right! _
I'm go-in' way down south, _
way down where I
Hey,
Joe,
where you gon - na
E
C
Gadd9
can be free!
Ain't no one gon-na find me babe!
Ain't no hang-man gon-na,
go?
Hey,

Dsus4
A
E
he ain't gon-na put a rope a - round me!
You bet - ter be - lieve it right
Joe, where you gon - na go?
now!
I got - ta go now!
Begin Fade
N.C.(C)
(G)
Hey, hey, hey, Joe,
Hey,
(D)
(A)
E
E7
you bet-ter run on down!
Good - bye ev-'ry-bod-y.
Ow!
Joe, where you gon-na go?
Fade Out
N.C.(C)
(G)
(D)
(A)
(E)
Hey, hey, Joe, what'd I say,
run on down!
(Hey,
Joe, where you gon - na go?)

I Can See for Miles

Words and Music by Peter Townshend

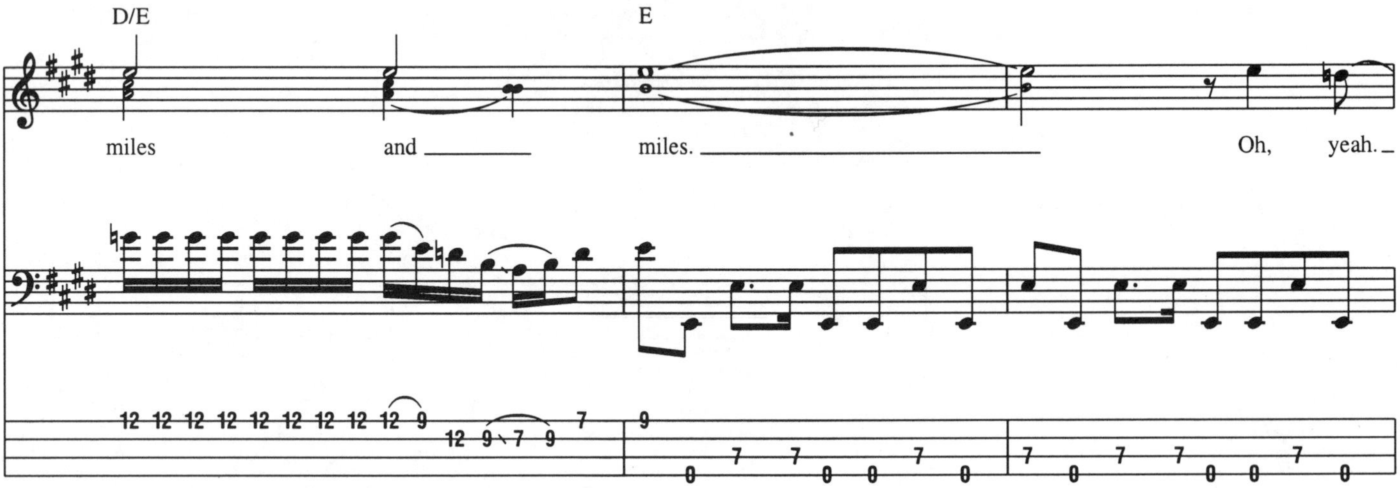
D/E
E
miles and miles. Oh, yeah.

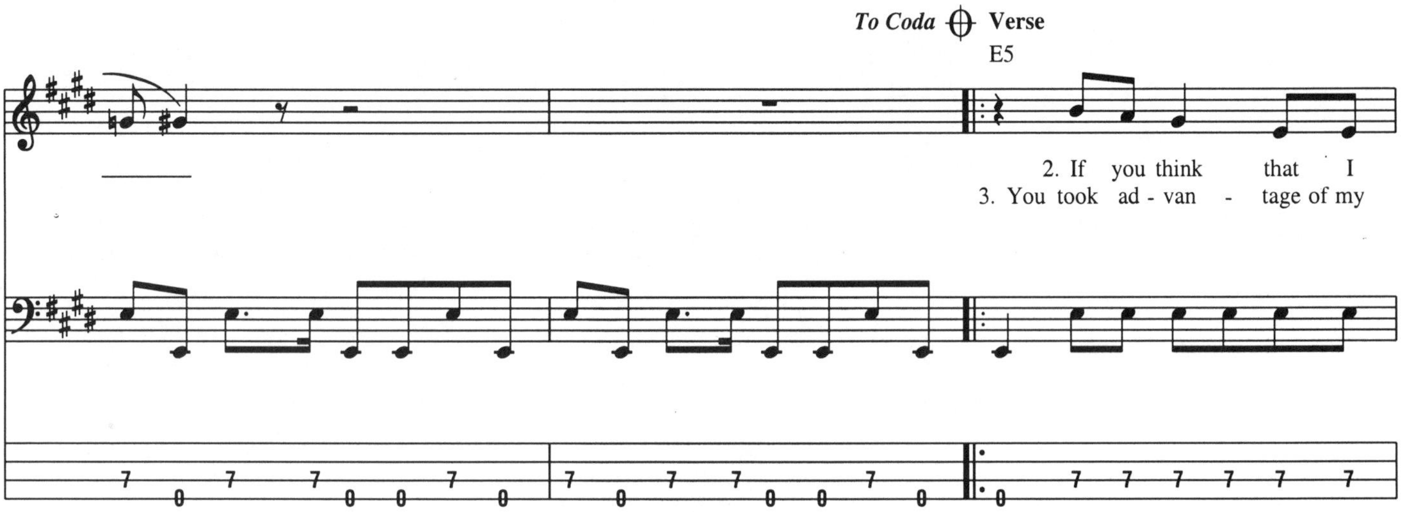
To Coda Verse
E5
2. If you think that I
3. You took ad - van - tage of my

2nd time, w/ Bass Fill 1
G5 A5 E5 G5 A5
don't know a - bout the lit-tle tricks you play
trust in you when I was so far a - way.

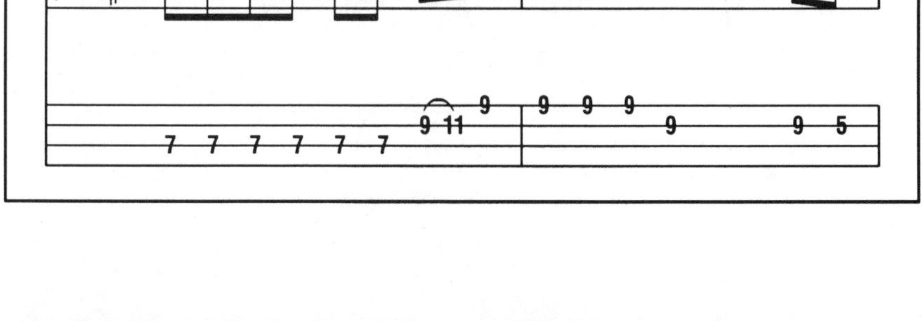
Bass Fill 1

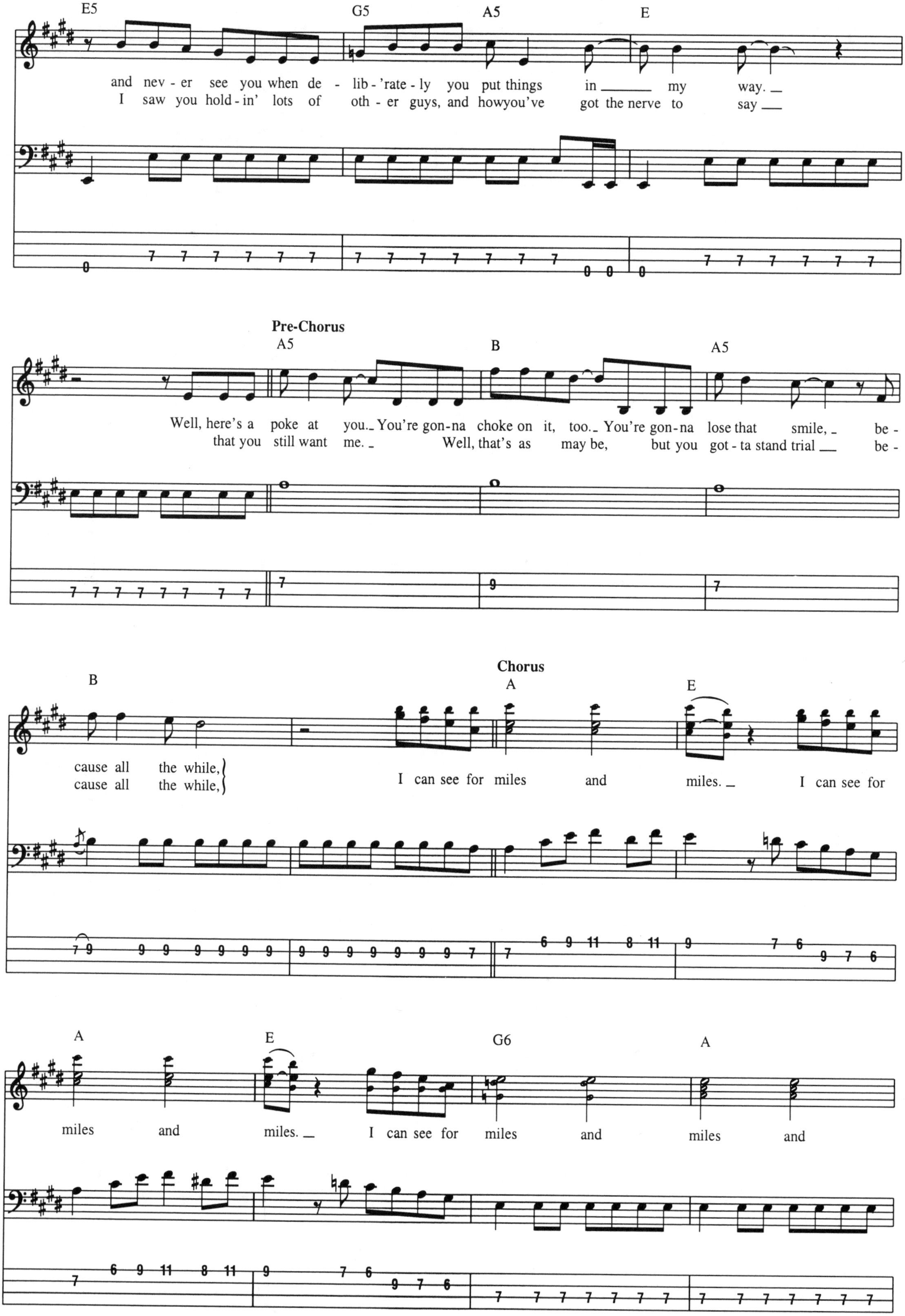
E5
G5
A5
E
and nev - er see you when de - lib - 'rate - ly you put things in my way.
I saw you hold - in' lots of oth - er guys, and howyou've got the nerve to say
Pre-Chorus
A5
B
A5
Well, here's a poke at you. You're gon-na choke on it, too. You're gon-na lose that smile, be -
that you still want me. Well, that's as may be, but you got - ta stand trial be -
B
Chorus
A
E
cause all the while,
cause all the while,
I can see for miles and miles. I can see for
A
E
G6
A
miles and miles. I can see for miles and miles and

C
D/E
E
miles and miles and miles.
Oh, yeah.
1.
2.
Guitar Solo
E5
G5
A5
D.S. al Coda
4. I

Coda
Verse
A5
C5
D5
A5
5. The Eif - fel Tow - er and the Taj Ma - hal are mine to see on clear _ days. _
C5
D5
A5
C5
D5
You thought that I __ would need a crys - tal ball to see right
A5
Pre-Chorus
D
E5
through the haze. _ Well here's a poke at you. _ You're gon-na choke on it, too. _ You're gon-na
Dsus2
E5
Chorus
D5
E5
lose that smile, _ be - cause all _ the while, I can see for miles and

A5
D5
E5
A5
C/A
miles. I can see for miles and miles. I can see for miles and
D/A
F/A
G/A
miles and miles and miles and miles and
miles and miles and miles.
A5
Repeat and fade
D5
E5
A5
I can see for miles and miles. I can see for

I Want You to Want Me

Words and Music by Rick Nielsen

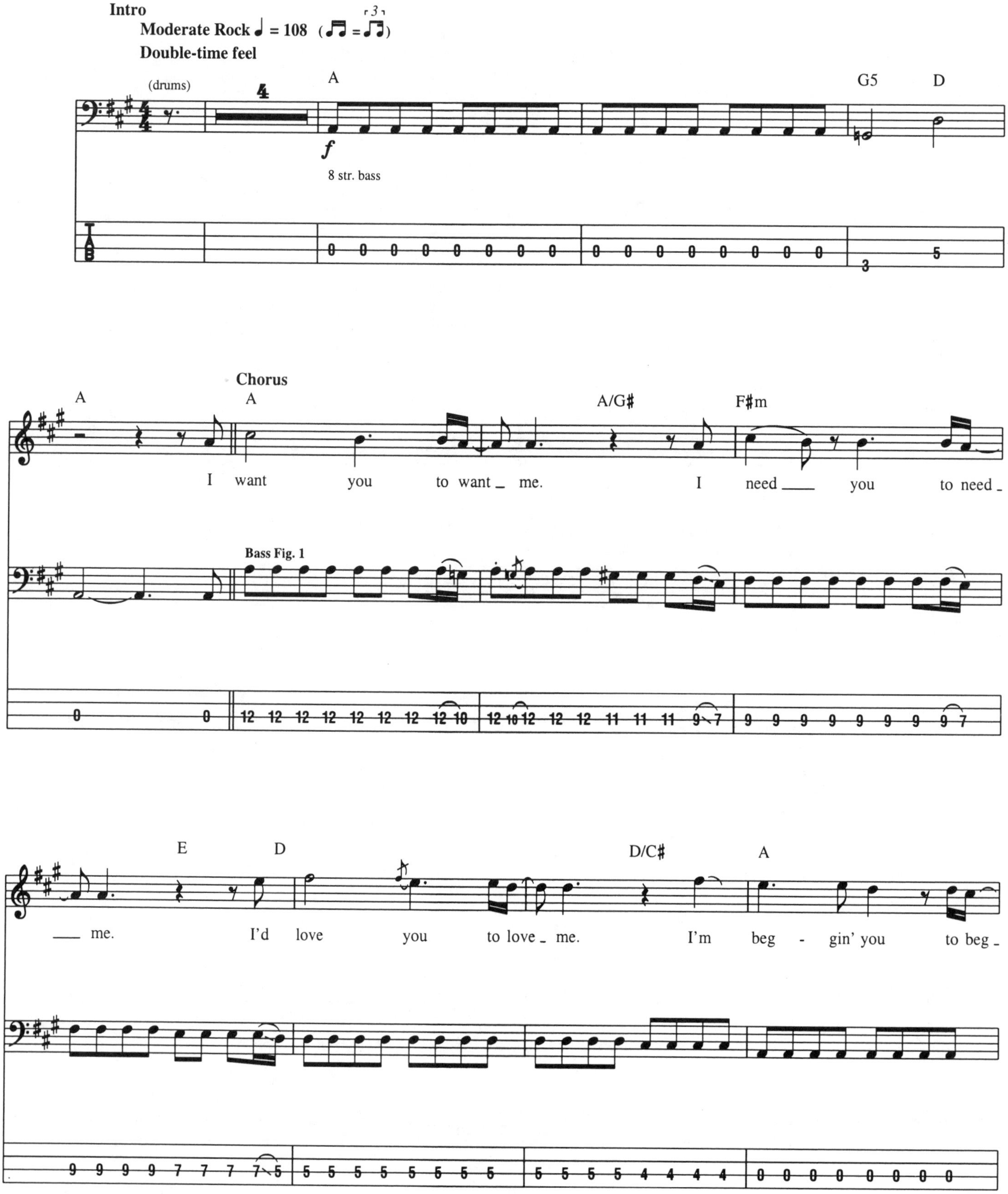

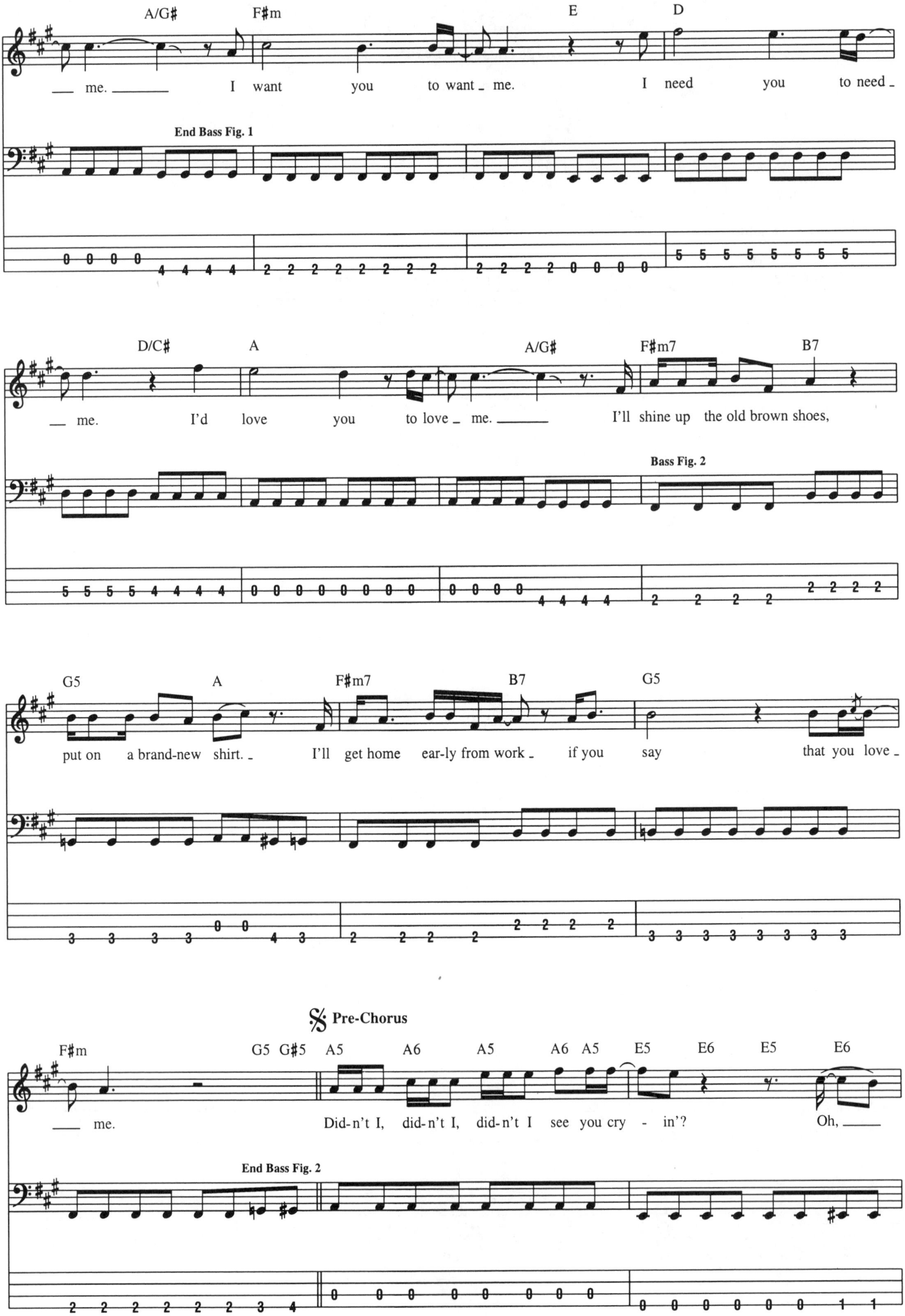
A/G♯ F♯m E D
me. I want you to want me. I need you to need
End Bass Fig. 1
D/C♯ A A/G♯ F♯m7 B7
me. I'd love you to love me. I'll shine up the old brown shoes,
Bass Fig. 2
G5 A F♯m7 B7 G5
put on a brand-new shirt. I'll get home ear-ly from work if you say that you love
Pre-Chorus
F♯m G5 G♯5 A5 A6 A5 A6 A5 E5 E6 E5 E6
me. Did-n't I, did-n't I, did-n't I see you cry - in'? Oh,
End Bass Fig. 2

2nd time, w/ Bass Fill 1
F♯m D A5 A6 A5 A6 A5
did-n't I, did-n't I, did-n't I see you cry - in'? Feel-in' all a-lone with-out a friend, you know you feel like dy-
2 2 2 2 2 2 2 2
5 5 5 5 5 4 3 2
0 0 0 0 0 0 0 0

To Coda
E5 E6 E5 E6 F♯m D
- in'. Oh, did-n't I, did-n't I, did-n't I see you cry - in'?
0 0 0 0 0 0 1 1
2 2 2 2 2 2 2 2
5 5 5 5 5 4 3 0

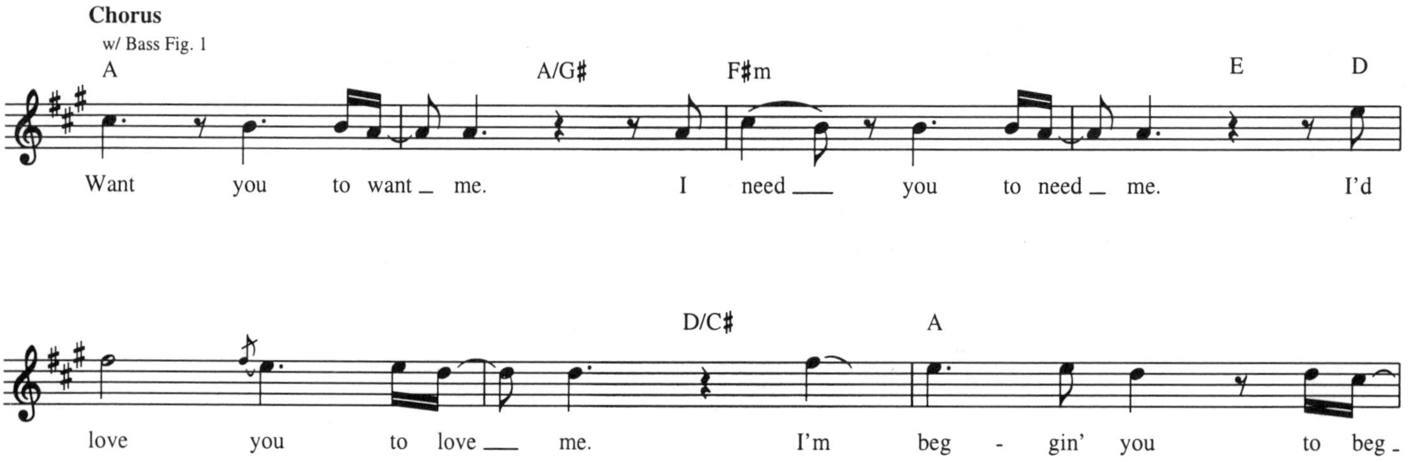
Chorus
w/ Bass Fig. 1
A A/G♯ F♯m E D
Want you to want me. I need you to need me. I'd
D/C♯ A
love you to love me. I'm beg - gin' you to beg -

Fill 1
5 5 5 5 5 5 5 5

w/ Bass Fig. 2
A/G# F#m B7 G5 A
me. I'll shine up the old brown shoes, put on a brand-new shirt. I'll
D.S. al Coda
F#m7 B7 G5 F#m G5 G#5
get home ear - ly from work if you say that you love me.
Coda
Guitar Solo
A5 A6 A5 A6 A5 E5 E6 E5 E6
- in'? Oh.
Pre-Chorus
F#m D A5 A6 A7 A6 A5 A6 A7 A6
Feel-in' all a-lone with-out a friend, you know you feel like dy -
E5 E6 E7 E6 E5 E6 F#m D
- in'. Oh, did-n't I, did-n't I, did-n't I see you cry - in'? Oh.

Guitar Solo
A E F#m D
I
0 0 0 0 0 0 0 0 0 0 0 0 0 0 1 1 2 2 2 2 2 2 2 2 5 5 5 5 5 5 5 5 4 3 0
Chorus
w/ Bass Fig. 1
A A/G# F#m E
want you to want _ me. I need ___ you to need _ me. I'd
D D/C# A End double-time feel A/G#
love you to love _ me. I'm ___ beg - gin' you to beg _ me. ___ I
Breakdown
N.C.(A)
Bass tacet
want ___ you to want _ me. ___ I want ___ you to want _ me. ___ I
5 (5) X X
want ___ you to want _ me. I ___ want ___ you ___ to want _ me. ___
10 10 10 10 10
Outro
Double-time feel
N.C.(A)
End double-time feel Free time
G5 D A5
0 0 0 0 0 0 0 0 0 0 0 0 0 0 0 0 3 5 0

Jerry Was a Race Car Driver

Lyrics by Les Claypool
Music by Les Claypool, Larry LaLonde and Tim Alexander

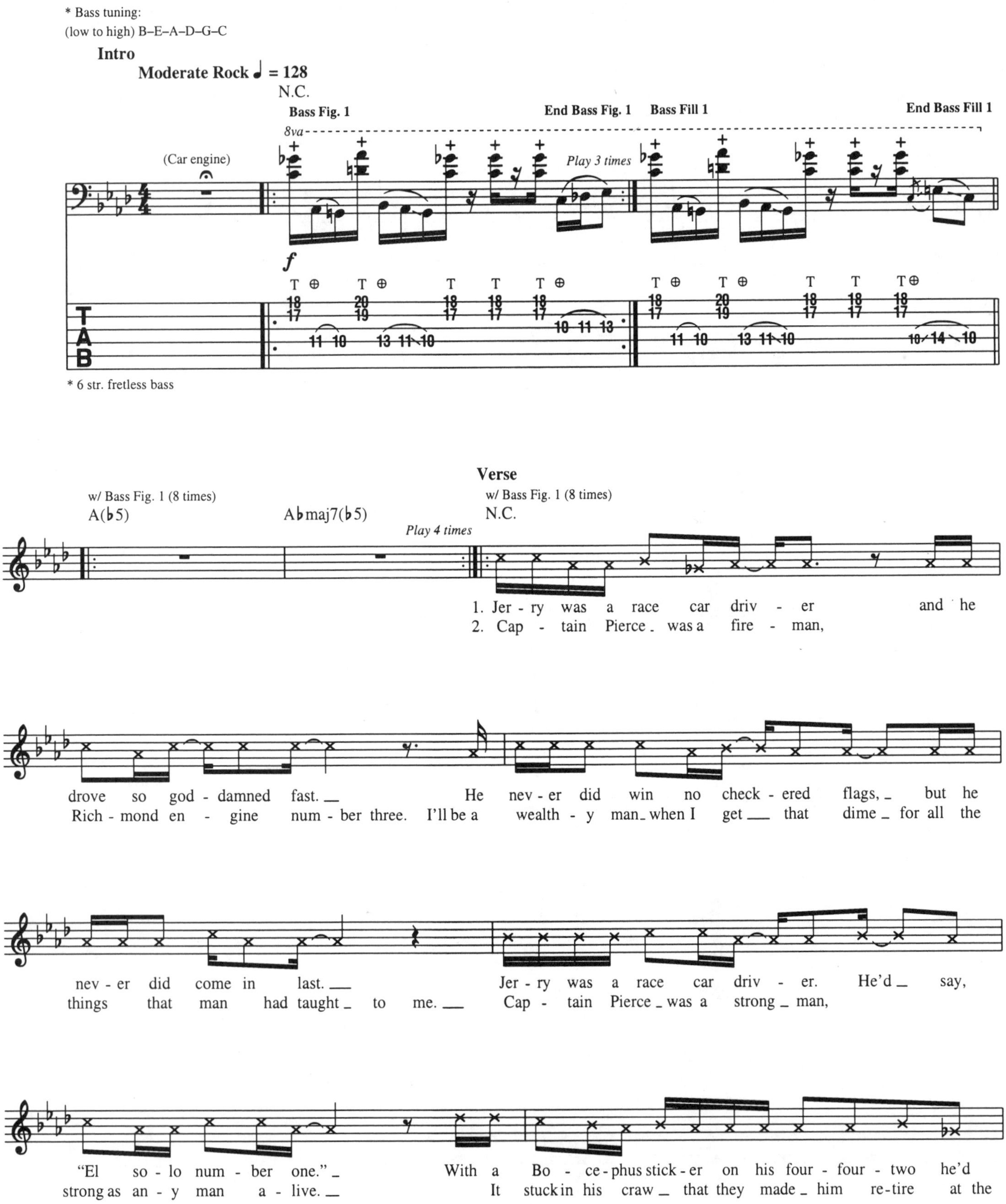

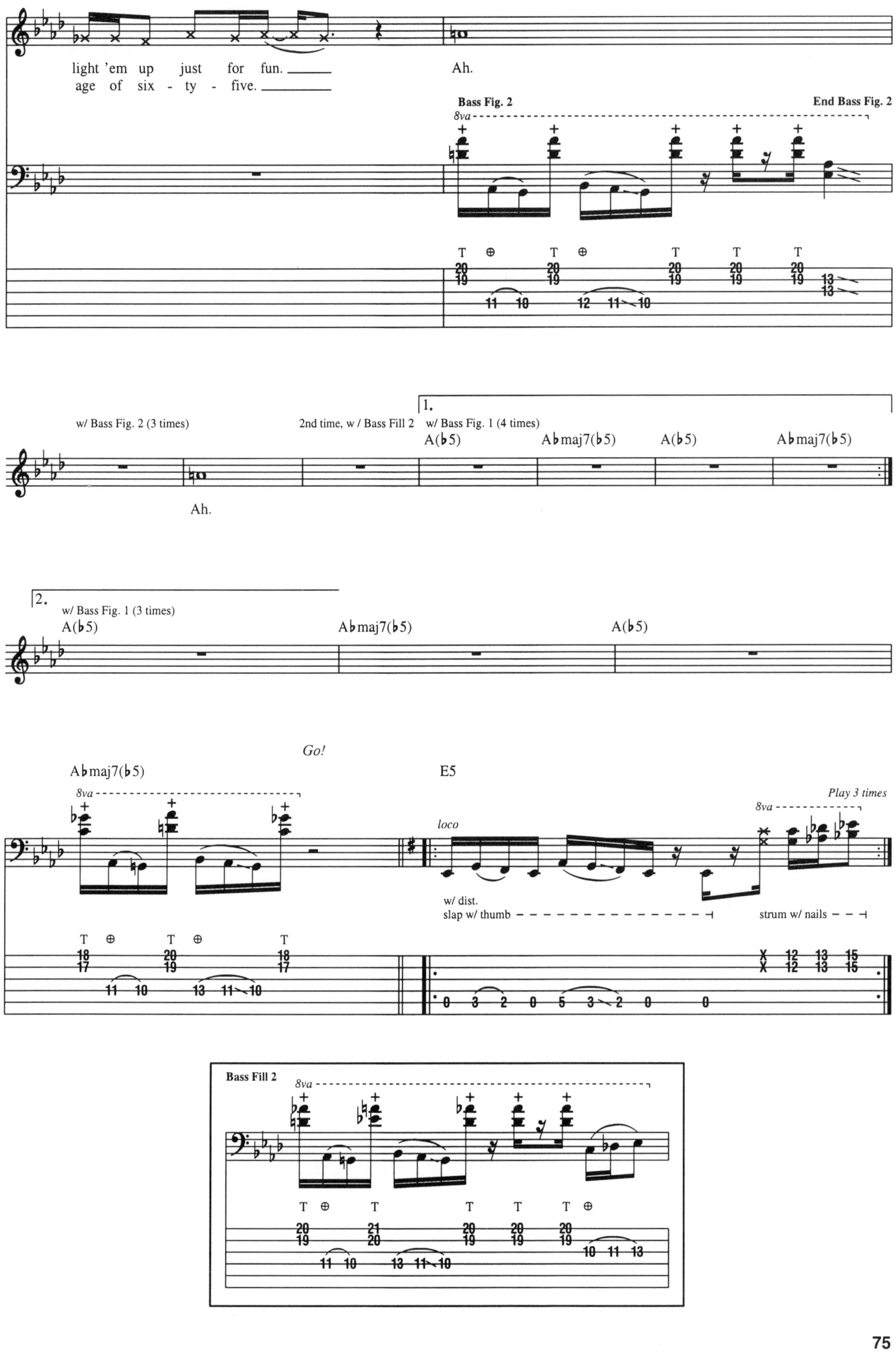
light 'em up just for fun.
age of six - ty - five.
Ah.
Bass Fig. 2
End Bass Fig. 2
8va
w/ Bass Fig. 2 (3 times)
2nd time, w / Bass Fill 2
1.
w/ Bass Fig. 1 (4 times)
A(♭5)
A♭maj7(♭5)
Ah.
2.
w/ Bass Fig. 1 (3 times)
Go!
E5
loco
Play 3 times
w/ dist.
slap w/ thumb
strum w/ nails
Bass Fill 2

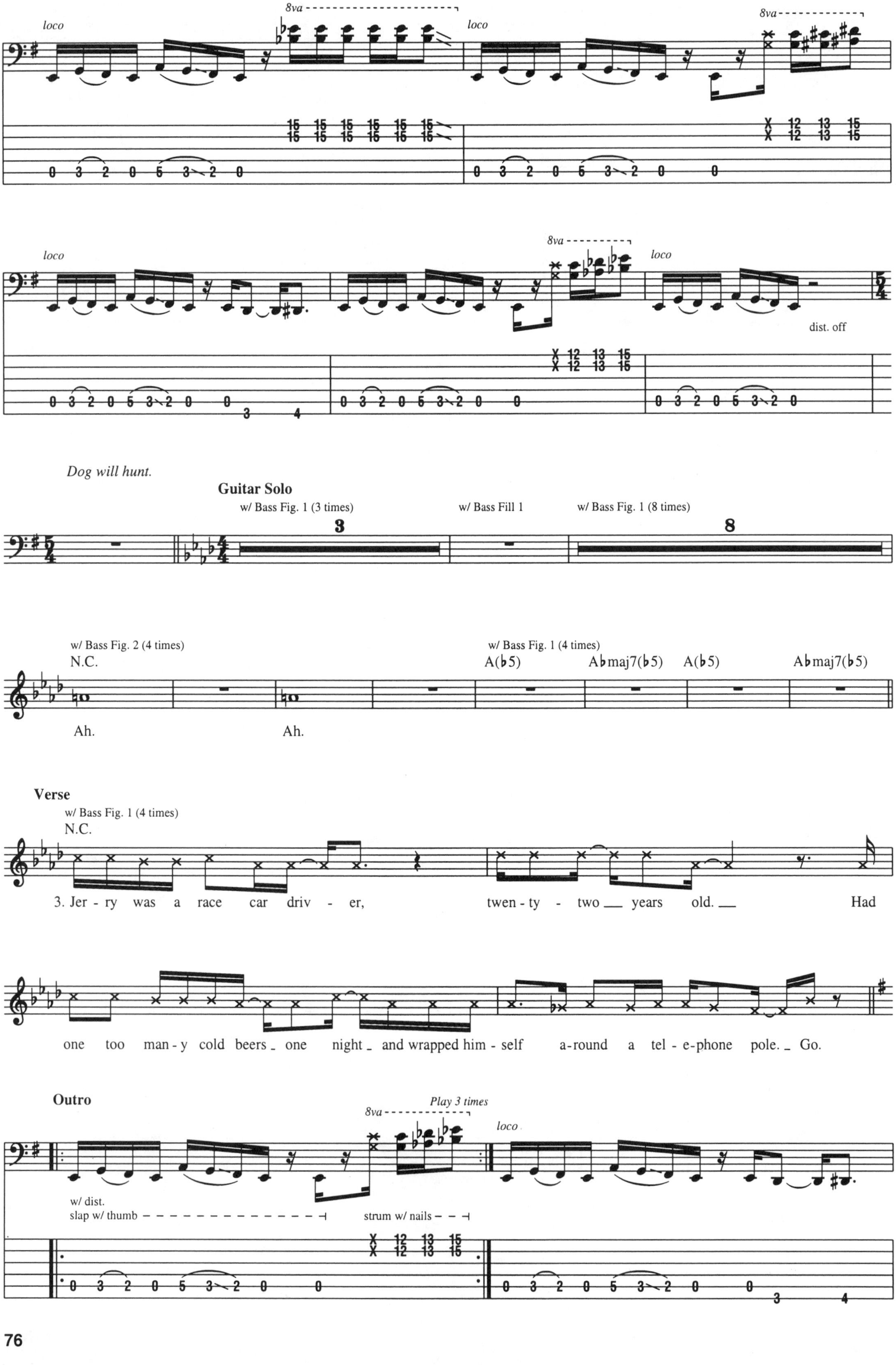
loco
8va
loco
8va
loco
8va
loco
dist. off
Dog will hunt.
Guitar Solo
w/ Bass Fig. 1 (3 times)
3
w/ Bass Fill 1
w/ Bass Fig. 1 (8 times)
8
w/ Bass Fig. 2 (4 times)
N.C.
w/ Bass Fig. 1 (4 times)
A(♭5) A♭maj7(♭5) A(♭5) A♭maj7(♭5)
Ah. Ah.
Verse
w/ Bass Fig. 1 (4 times)
N.C.
3. Jer - ry was a race car driv - er, twen - ty - two years old. Had
one too man - y cold beers one night and wrapped him - self a-round a tel - e-phone pole. Go.
Outro
Play 3 times
8va
loco
w/ dist.
slap w/ thumb
strum w/ nails

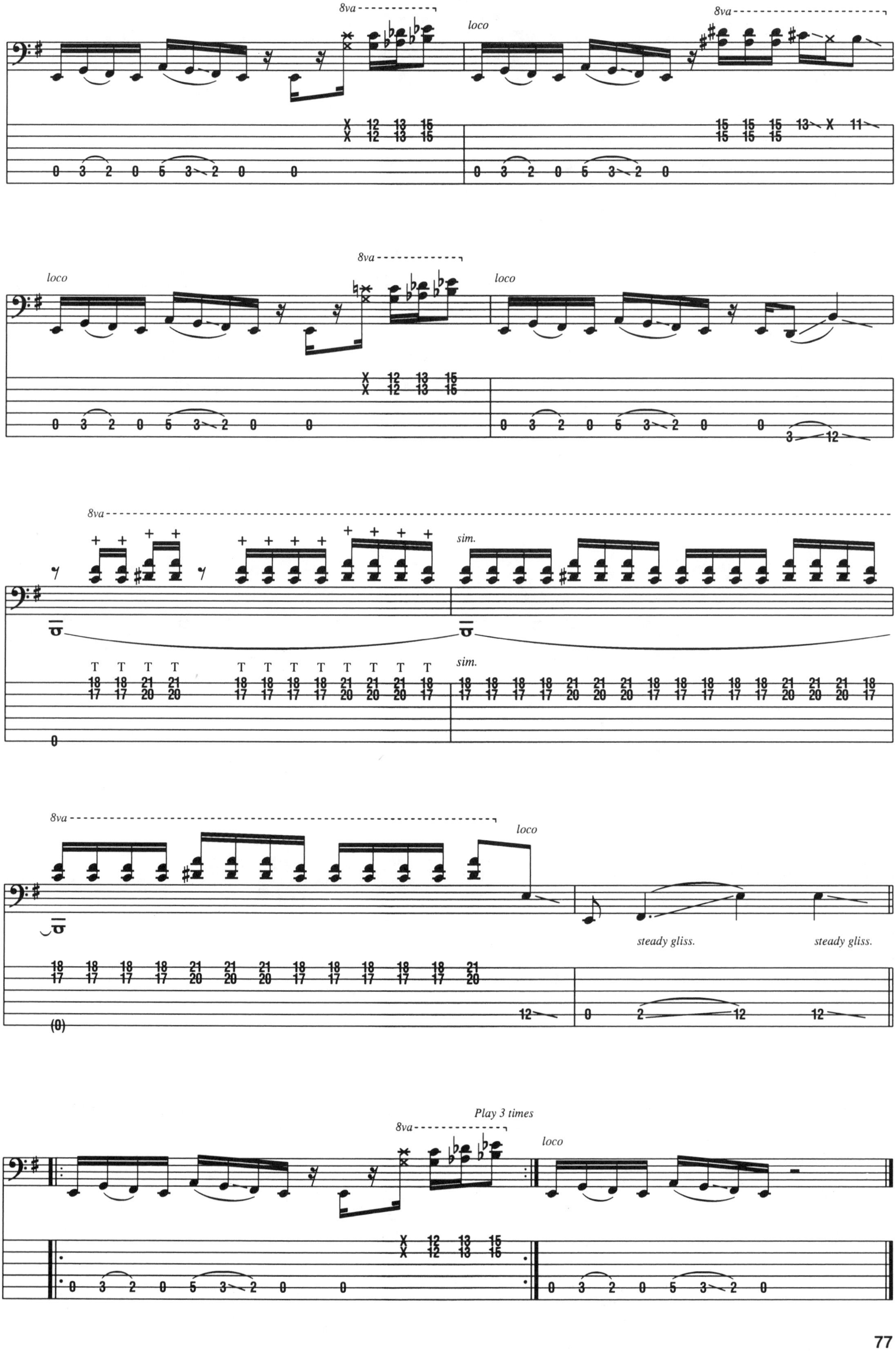
8va
loco
8va
loco
8va
loco
loco
8va
sim.
T
sim.
8va
loco
steady gliss.
steady gliss.
Play 3 times
8va
loco

Jessica

Written by Dickey Betts

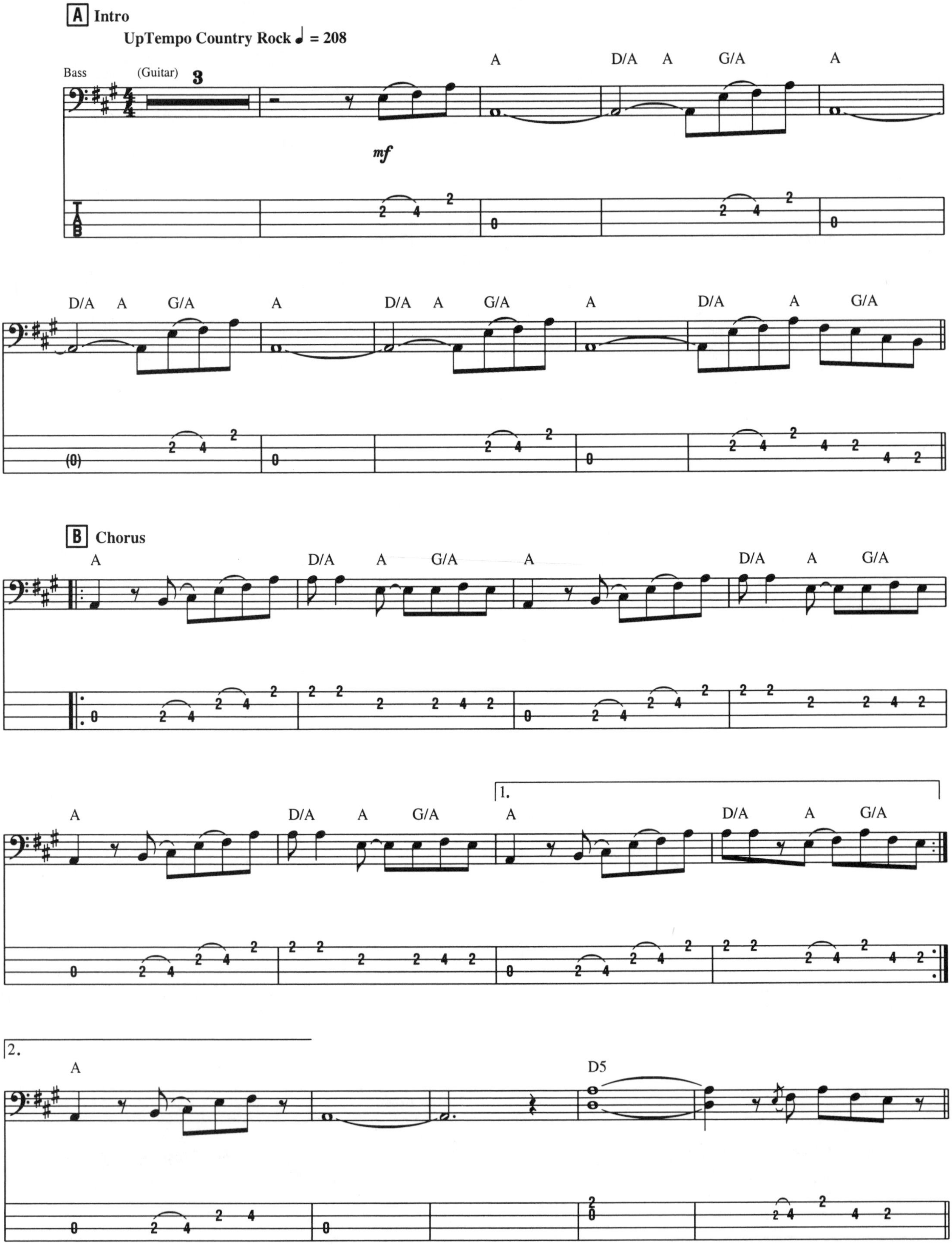

C Chorus
A
D/A A G/A
A
D/A A G/A
A
D/A A G/A
A
1.
D/A A G/A
2.
D/A A G/A
3
D Bridge
G
A
G
A
G
E
E Chorus
A
D/A A G/A
A
D/A A G/A
A
D/A A G/A
1.
A
D/A A G/A
2.
N.C.

F Breakdown
23
A
D/A
1.
2.
G Piano Solo
D
play 16 times
N.C.

H **Guitar Solo**

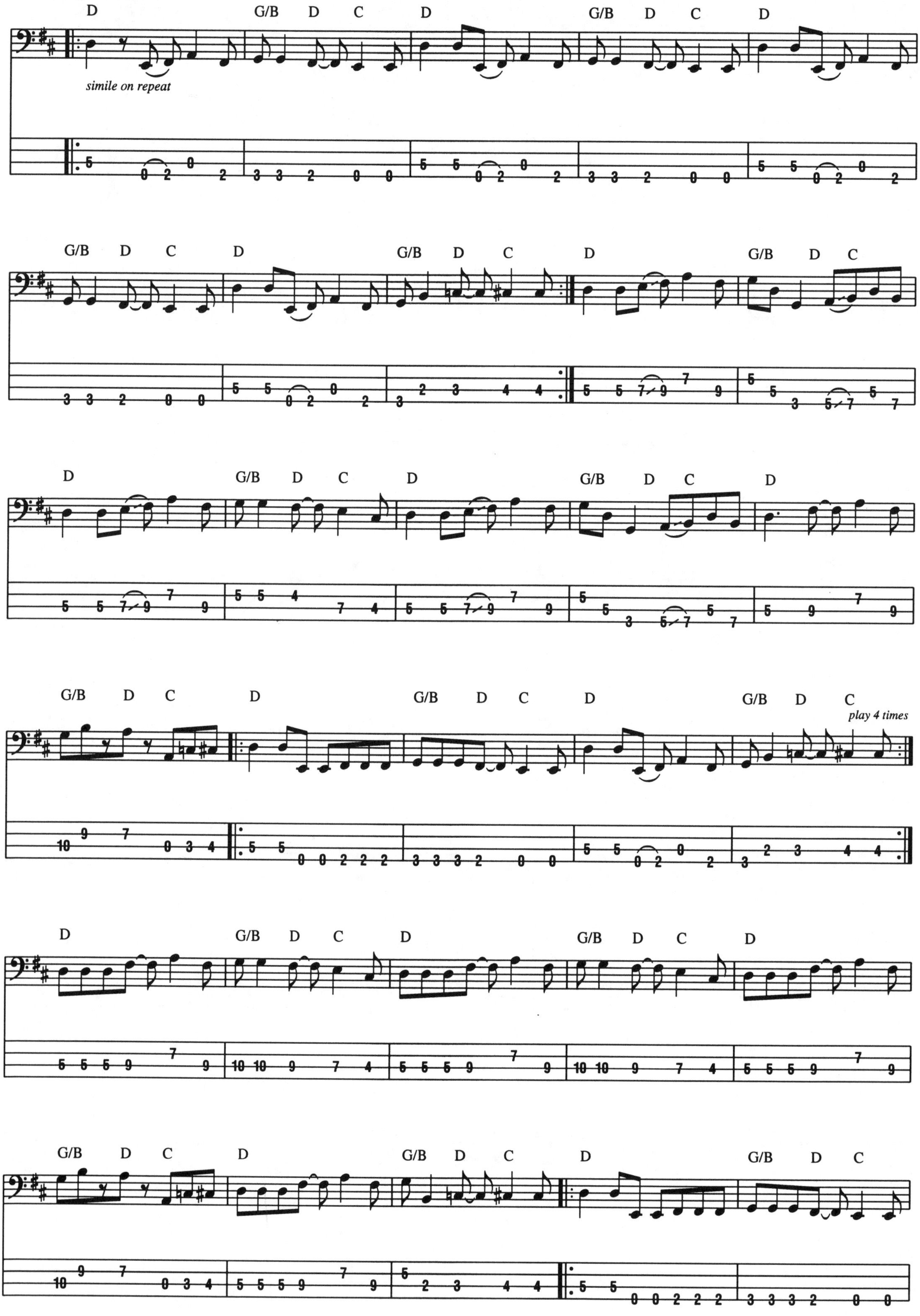

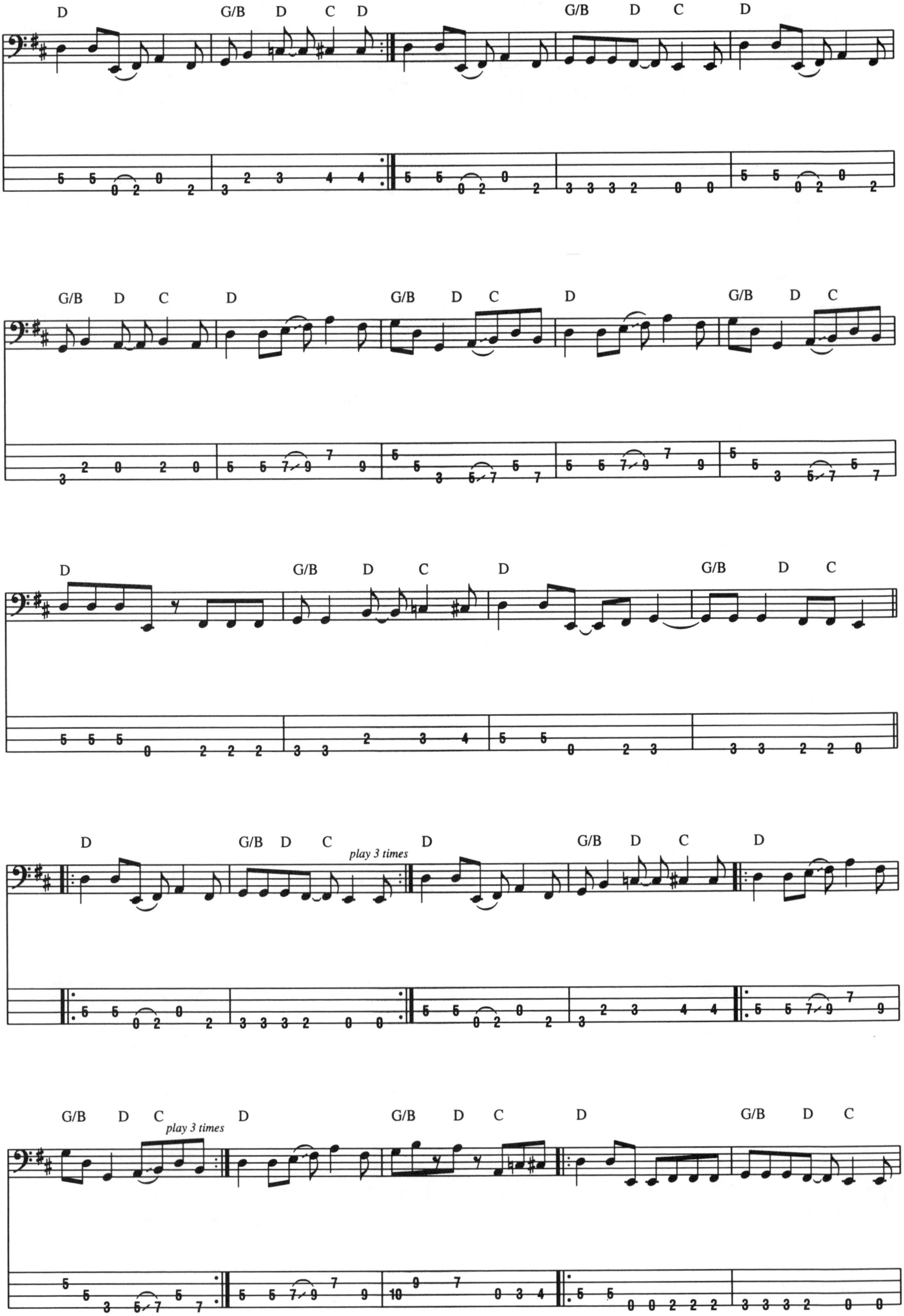
D
G/B D C D
G/B D C
D
play 3 times

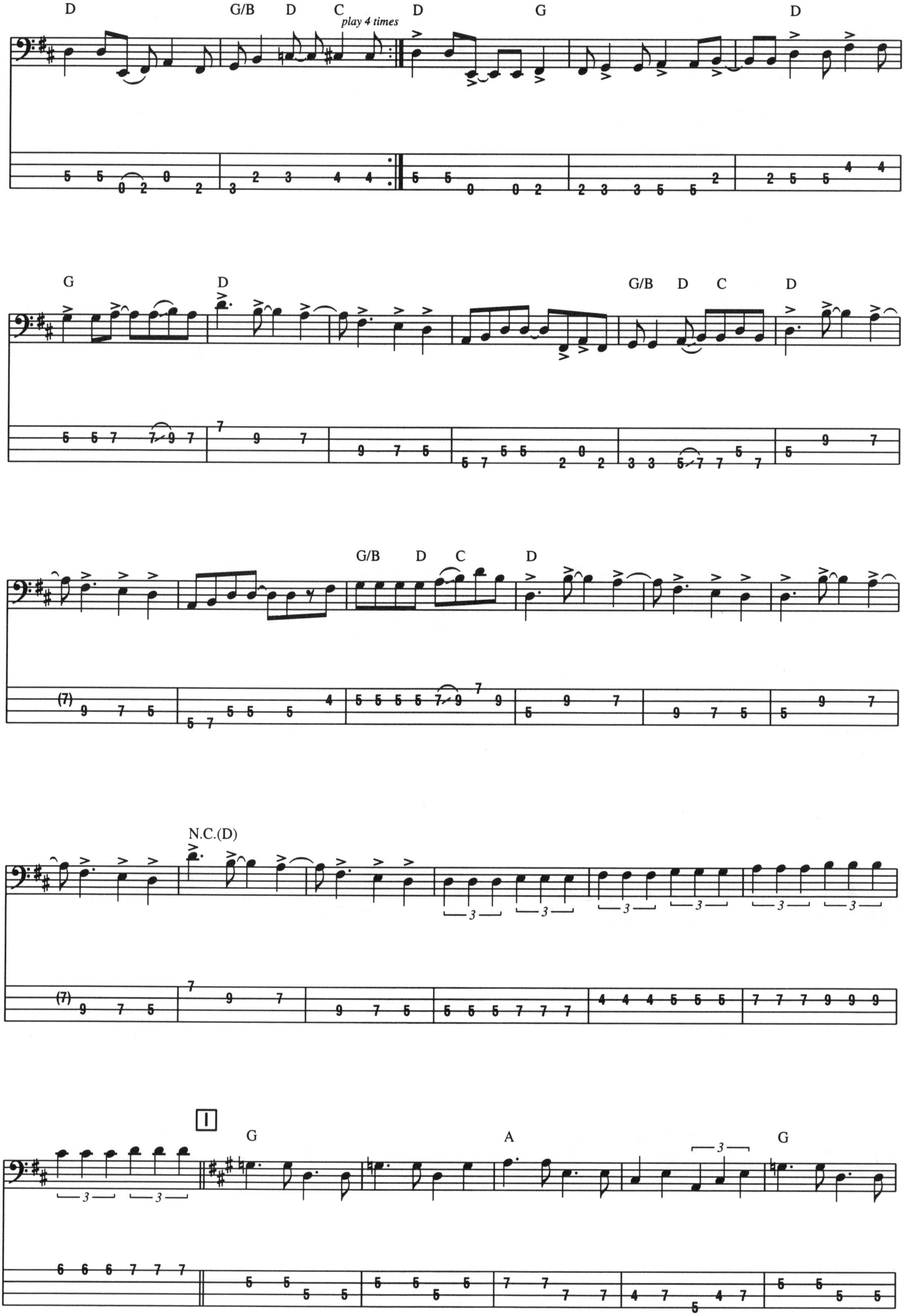
D
G/B
D
C
play 4 times
G
N.C.(D)
I
A

A
G
A
G
E
J Chorus
A
D/A A G/A
A
D/A A G/A
A
D/A A G/A
1., 3.
2.
4.
K Outro
Free Time
A
D/A A G/A
D/A A G/A
D/A A G/A
G
A

Living After Midnight

Words and Music by Glenn Tipton, Robert Halford and K.K. Downing

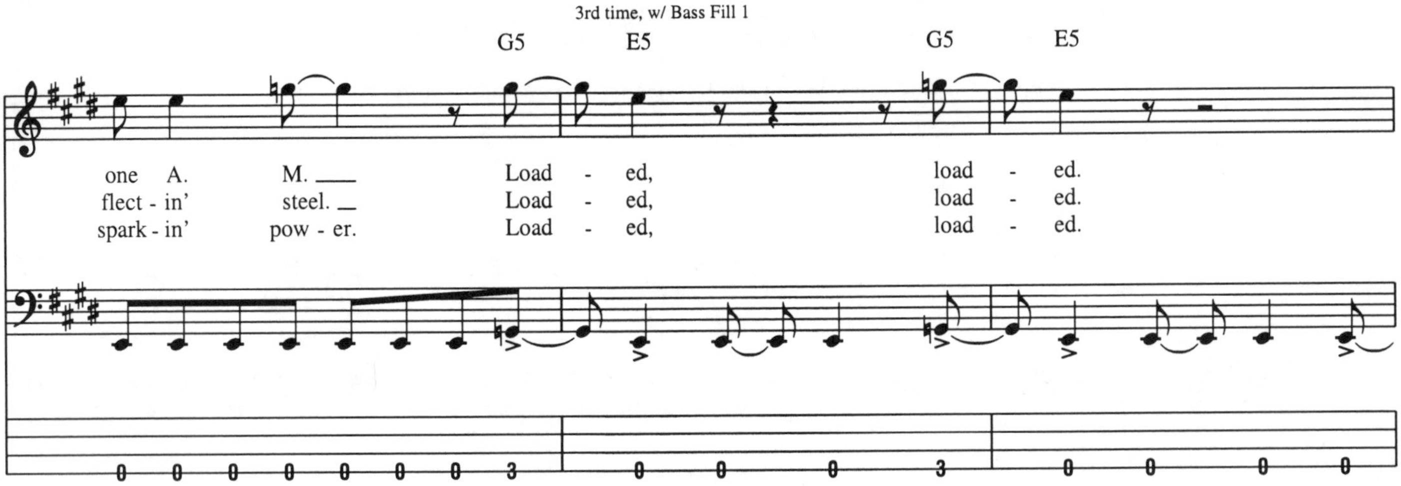
3rd time, w/ Bass Fill 1
G5
E5
G5
E5
one A. M. Load - ed, load - ed.
flect - in' steel. Load - ed, load - ed.
spark - in' pow - er. Load - ed, load - ed.

3rd time, w/ Bass Fill 1
G5
E5
G5
I'm all geared up to score a - gain. Load - ed, load -
Read - y to take on ev - 'ry deal. Load - ed, load -
I'm get - ting hard - er by the hour. Load - ed, load -

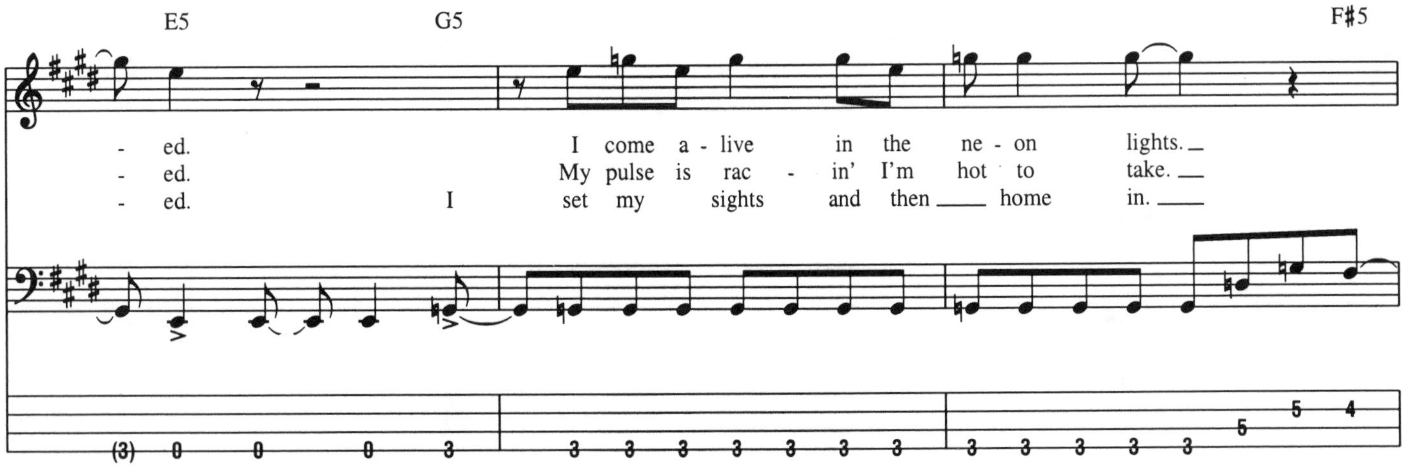
E5
G5
F♯5
- ed. I come a - live in the ne - on lights.
- ed. My pulse is rac - in' I'm hot to take.
- ed. I set my sights and then home in.

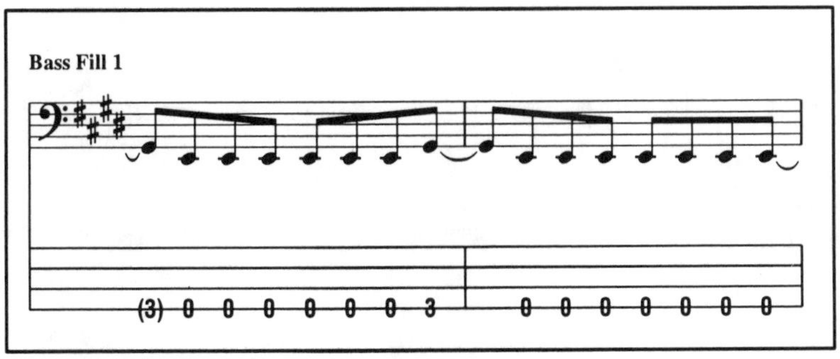
Bass Fill 1

Chorus
B5 D5 E D A
That's when I make my moves right.
This motor's revved up, fit to break
The joint starts fly'n' when I begin.
Living after
B E D A B E D A
midnight, rockin' to the dawn. Lovin' till the
To Coda
1.
2.
B E5 A
mornin', then I'm gone, I'm gone.
Bridge
D/A A D/A A E5 G5 E5 A
I'm aimin' for ya.

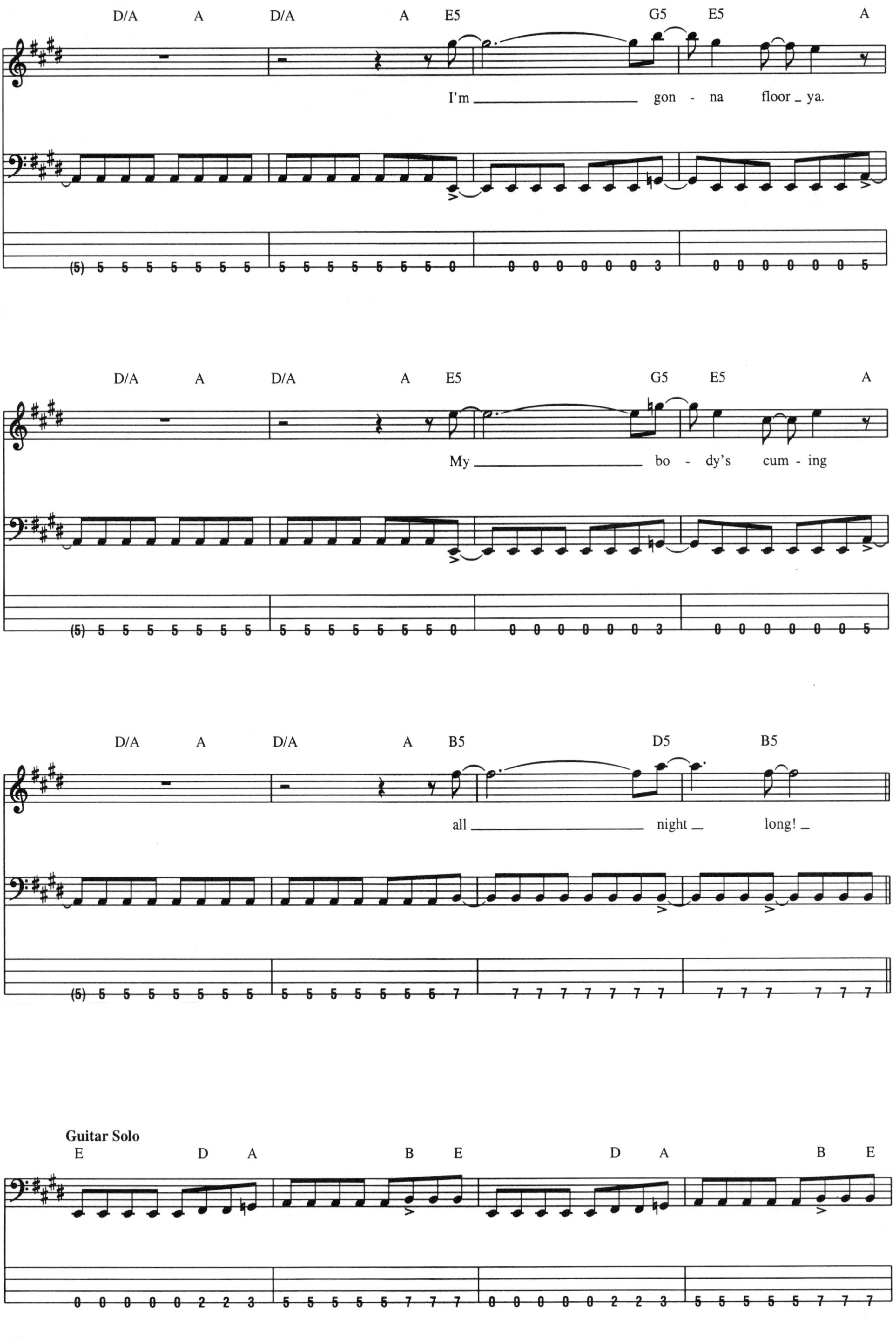
D/A A D/A A E5 G5 E5 A
I'm gon - na floor ya.
D/A A D/A A E5 G5 E5 A
My bo - dy's cum - ing
D/A A D/A A B5 D5 B5
all night long!
Guitar Solo
E D A B E D A B E

D.S. al Coda
E D A B E
0 0 0 0 0 2 2 3 5 5 5 5 5 7 7 7 7 7 7 7 7 7 7 7 7 7 7 7 0
Coda
Outro-Chorus
E D A B E
Liv - ing af - ter mid - night,
(7) 7 7 7 7 7 7 7 0 0 0 0 0 0 2 3 5 5 5 5 5 7 7 7
D A B E D A
rock - in' to the dawn. Lov - in' till the
0 0 0 0 0 2 3 5 5 5 5 5 7 7 7 0 0 0 0 0 2 3
Repeat and fade
B E
morn - in', then I'm gone, I'm gone.
5 5 5 5 5 7 7 7 7 7 7 7 7 7 7 7 7 7 7 7 7

The Loco-Motion

Words and Music by Gerry Goffin and Carole King

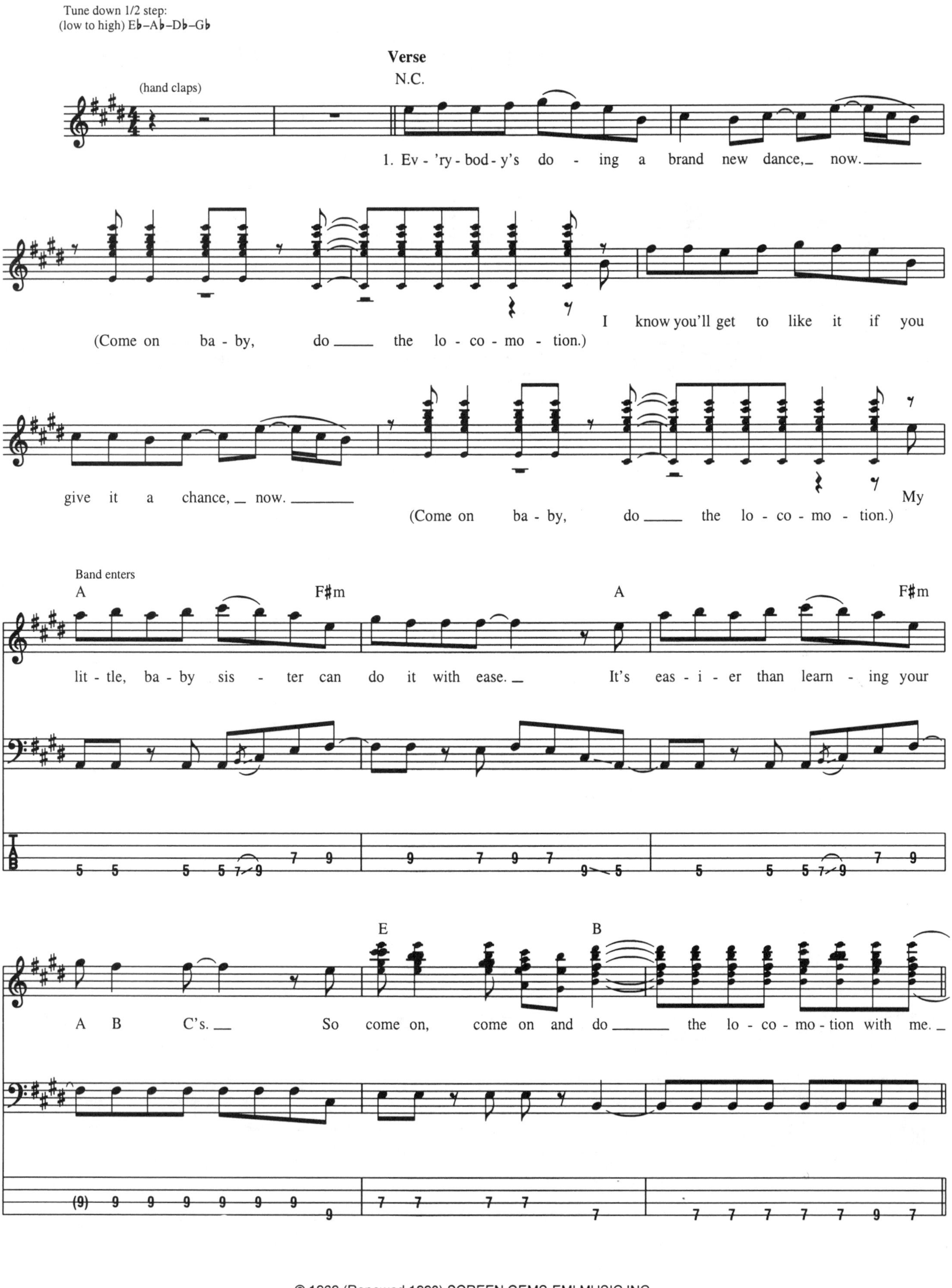
Tune down 1/2 step:
(low to high) E♭–A♭–D♭–G♭
Verse
N.C.
(hand claps)
1. Ev - 'ry - bod - y's do - ing a brand new dance, now.
(Come on ba - by, do the lo - co - mo - tion.)
I know you'll get to like it if you
give it a chance, now.
(Come on ba - by, do the lo - co - mo - tion.)
My
Band enters
A
F♯m
lit - tle, ba - by sis - ter can do it with ease.
It's eas - i - er than learn - ing your
E
B
A B C's.
So come on, come on and do the lo - co - mo - tion with me.

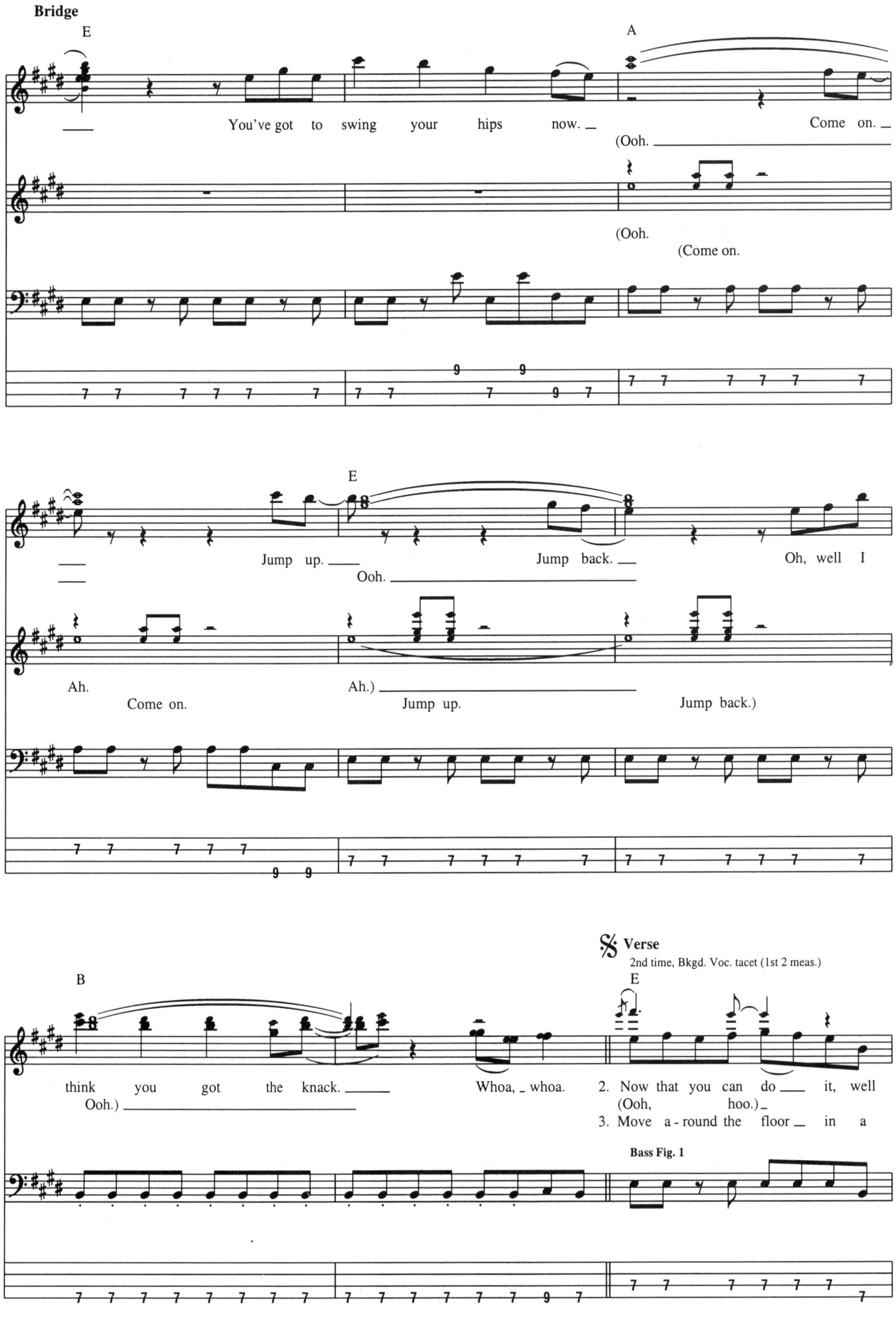
Bridge
E
A
You've got to swing your hips now.
Come on.
(Ooh.
(Ooh.
(Come on.
E
Jump up.
Jump back.
Oh, well I
Ooh.
Ah.
Come on.
Ah.)
Jump up.
Jump back.)
Verse
2nd time, Bkgd. Voc. tacet (1st 2 meas.)
B
E
think you got the knack.
Ooh.)
Whoa, whoa.
2. Now that you can do it, well
(Ooh, hoo.)
3. Move a-round the floor in a
Bass Fig. 1

C#m
E
C#m
let's make a chain, now.
lo - co - mo - tion.
(Come on ba - by, do the lo - co - mo - tion.)
A
End Bass Fig. 1
w/ Bass Fig. 1
E
C#m
E
chug - a, chug - a mo - tion like a rail - road train, now.
Do it hold - ing hands if - 'n you get the no - tion.
(Come on ba - by, do
A
F#m
Do it nice and eas - y now and don't lose con - trol.
There's nev - er been a dance that's so eas - y to do.
the lo - co - mo - tion.)
A
It
To Coda
A
F#
E
B
lit - tle, bit of rhy - thm and a lot of soul.
e - ven makes you hap - py when you're feel - ing blue.
So come on, come on and do the lo - co - mo - tion with me.
* Bkgd. Voc. 1st time only

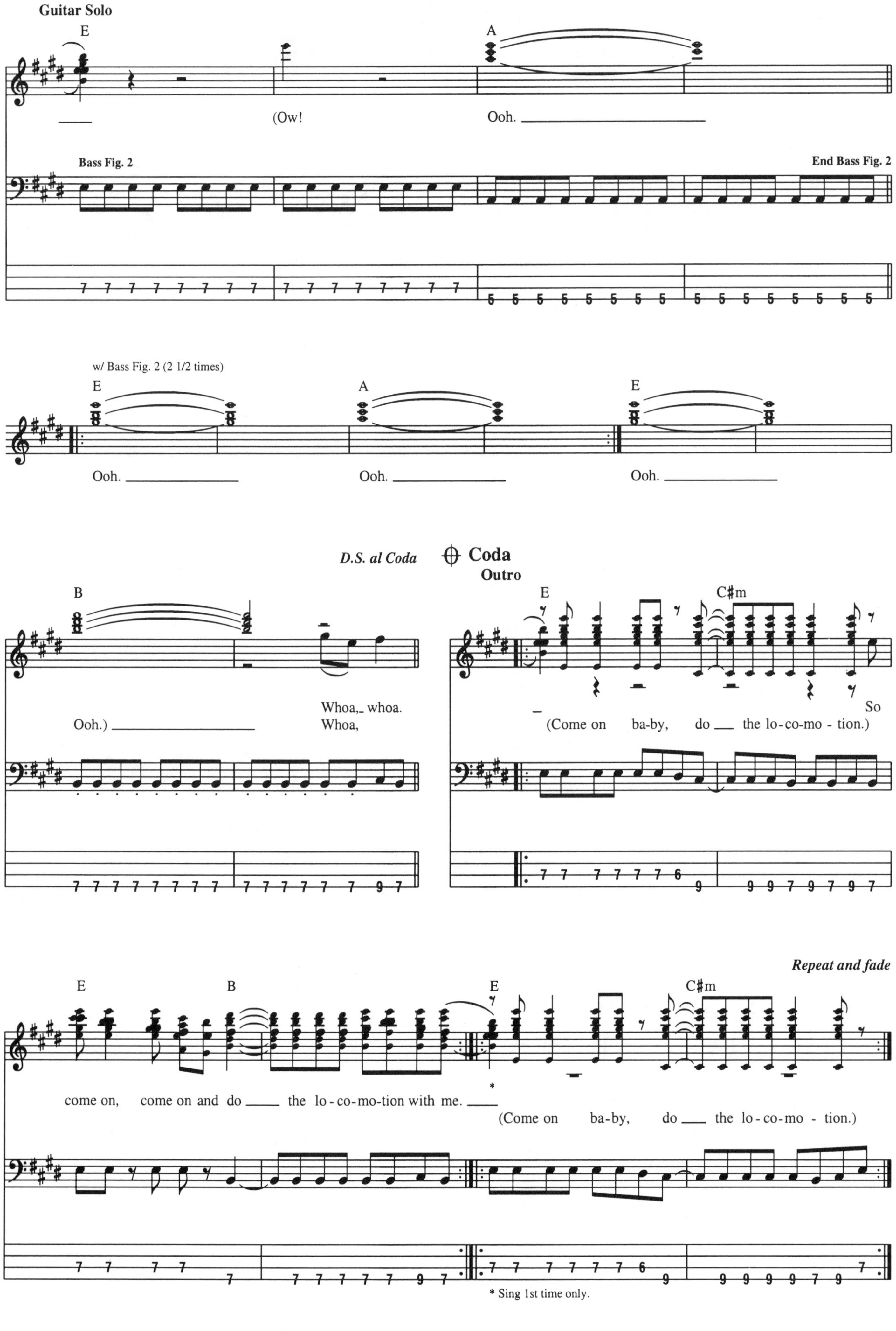

Guitar Solo
E
A
(Ow!
Ooh.
Bass Fig. 2
End Bass Fig. 2
w/ Bass Fig. 2 (2 1/2 times)
E
A
E
Ooh.
Ooh.
Ooh.
D.S. al Coda
Coda
Outro
B
Ooh.)
Whoa,_ whoa.
Whoa,
E
C#m
(Come on ba-by, do the lo-co-mo - tion.)
So
Repeat and fade
E
B
E
C#m
come on, come on and do the lo-co-mo-tion with me.
(Come on ba-by, do the lo-co-mo - tion.)
* Sing 1st time only.

Miss You

Words and Music by Mick Jagger and Keith Richards

Am
I've been hang-in' on the phone, I've been sleep-in' all a-lone. I wan-na
Chorus
Dm7
Am
kiss you some-time. Oo hoo oo, oo hoo oo, hoo
Dm7
Am
oo oo, now. Oo hoo oo, oo hoo oo, oo
Verse
Dm7
Am
oo oo, yah. 2. Well, I've been haunt - ed in my sleep, you been star-

Dm7
in' in my dreams. Lord, I miss you, child. I've been
(Spoken: Play it, Ron!)
Am
Dm7
wait-in' in the hall, been wait-in' on your call, when the phone rings. Spoken: It's just some friends
Am
of mine. They say, "Hey! What's the mat-ter man? We're gon-
Dm7
na come 'round at twelve with some Puer-to Ri-can girls that's just dy'n to

Am
meet you! We're gon - na bring a case of wine. Hey, let's go mess and fool a-round you know,
Dm7
Chorus
Am
like we used to!"
(Ah ah ah, ah ah ah, ah
Dm7
Am
ah ah.)
I say, well... Ah
(Ah ah ah, ah ah ah, ah
let ring
Dm7
Bridge
F
ah ah.
ah ah.)
Oh, oo, ba -
(Oo.

Em7
Dm7
by, why you wait so long
Yeah.
)
F
Em7
Dm7
Oh, ba - by, why you wait so long
Won't ya
(Oo.)
Interlude
E
N.C.(Am)
(Dm)
come home! Come home!
Spoken: Ahh...
T' t-'ck, t' t-'ck, t' t-'ck
(Spoken: Come home now, baby. Ya know what I'm sayin'...)
p
mp
(Am)
t' 'ck!
I've been walk-in' Cen-tral Park,
sing-in' af - ter dark.
Peo-ple think

(Dm)
(Am)
I'm cra - zy.
Stum-bl - in' on my feet,
shuff-lin' to the street.
(Dm)
Ask - in' me, "'Ch 'ch 'ch!
What's the mat-ter with you, boy?"
(Am)
(Dm)
Dm7
Some-time I wan-na say, to, to my-self...
Some-time I say...
Oo
Chorus
Am
Dm7
hoo oo, oo hoo oo, oo oo oo, yeah.
Oo
mf

Am
Dm7
oo _ oo, _ oo _ oo _ oo, _ I wan-na kiss you, child. _ Wow _
Saxophone Solo
Am
Dm7
Am
Dm7
3. I guess _ I'm ly -
Verse
Am
Dm7
in' to my-self, _ it's just you _ and no one else. _ Lord, _ I wan-na kiss you, child. _ You just been

Am
Dm7
blot-tin'out _ my mind, _ fool-in'on _ my time. _ Lord, I wan-na kiss _ you, ba - by, _ yeah. Lord, _
_ I miss you, child. _ Oo, _ hoo, _ ah, _ ah, ah, 'h!
(Ah _
Chorus
Uh, uh, uh! Huh, _ uh, _ uh! Lord, _ I miss you, child. _
ah _ ah, _ ah _ ah _ ah, _ ah _ ah ah. _)
(Ah _
Lord, _ I miss you, child. _
ah _ ah, _ ah _ ah _ ah, _ ah _ ah ah. _
(Ah _

Am
Dm7
Oo oo oo, oo hoo oo. Come on, Dave,. play it for me now!
ah ah, ah ah ah, ah ah ah.)
Harmonica Solo
Yeah!
Begin Fade
Fade Out

Money

Words and Music by Roger Waters

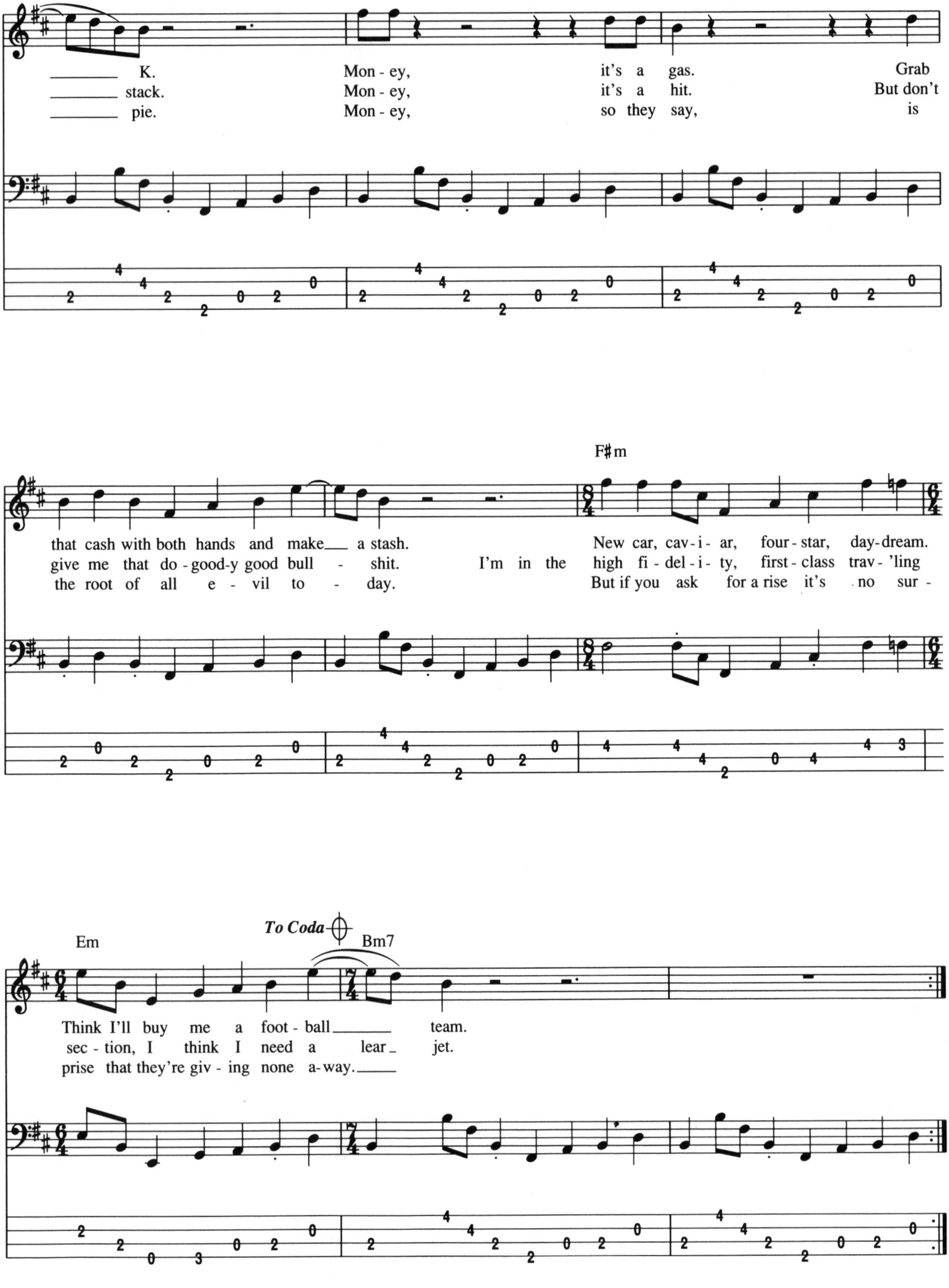
K.
stack.
pie.
Mon - ey,
Mon - ey,
Mon - ey,
it's a gas.
it's a hit.
so they say,
Grab
But don't
is
F♯m
that cash with both hands and make a stash.
give me that do - good-y good bull - shit.
the root of all e - vil to - day.
I'm in the
New car, cav - i - ar, four - star, day-dream.
high fi - del - i - ty, first - class trav - 'ling
But if you ask for a rise it's no sur -
Em
To Coda
Bm7
Think I'll buy me a foot - ball team.
sec - tion, I think I need a lear - jet.
prise that they're giv - ing none a-way.

B Sax Solo

C Guitar Solo

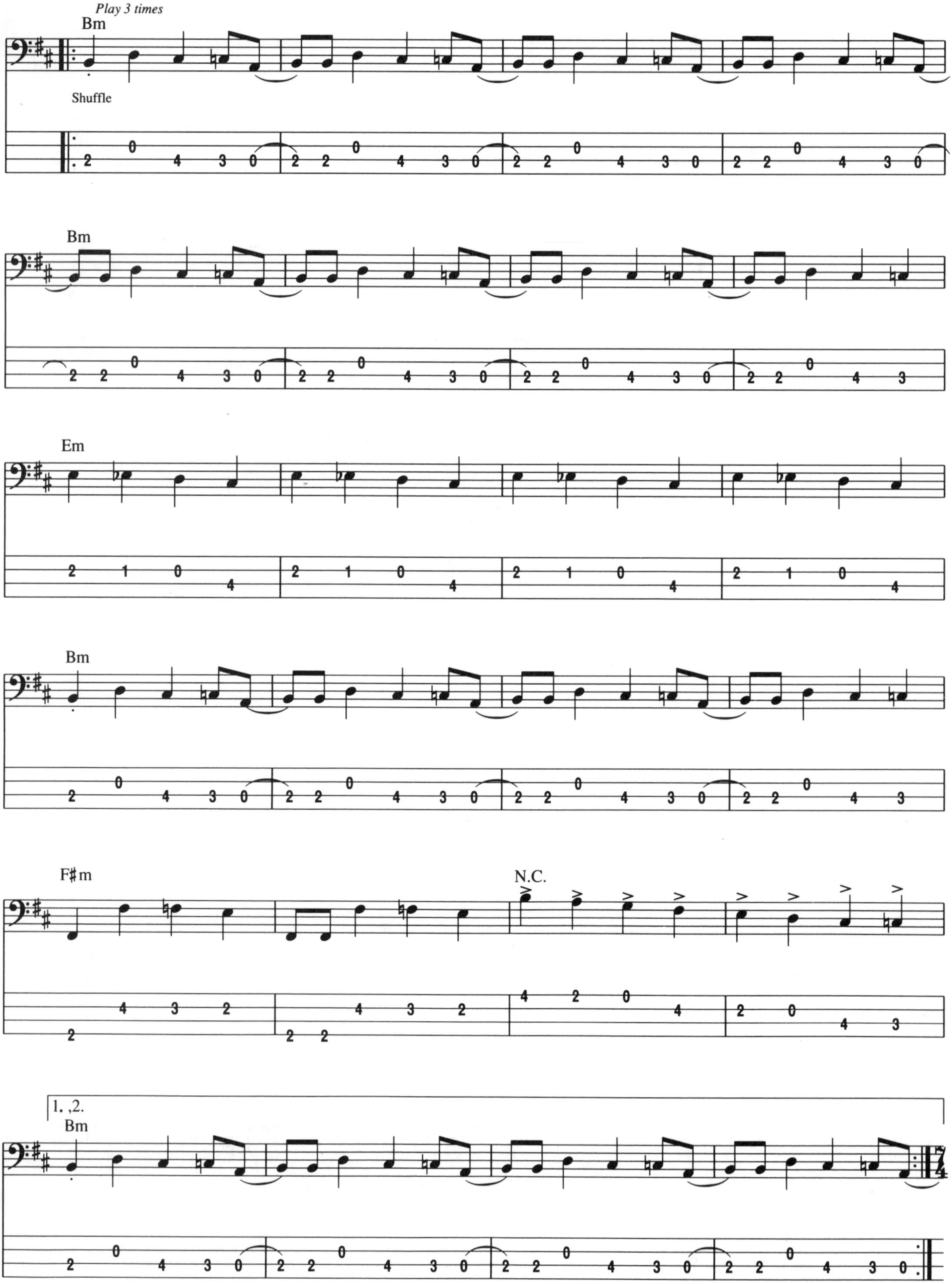

D.S. al Coda
3.
Bm
Coda
Bm7
(way), a - way, a - way, a - way,
a - way, a - way, a - way, a - way,
Ooh,
Segue
Background conversation fades in while the band fades out on this groove

My Generation

Words and Music by Peter Townshend

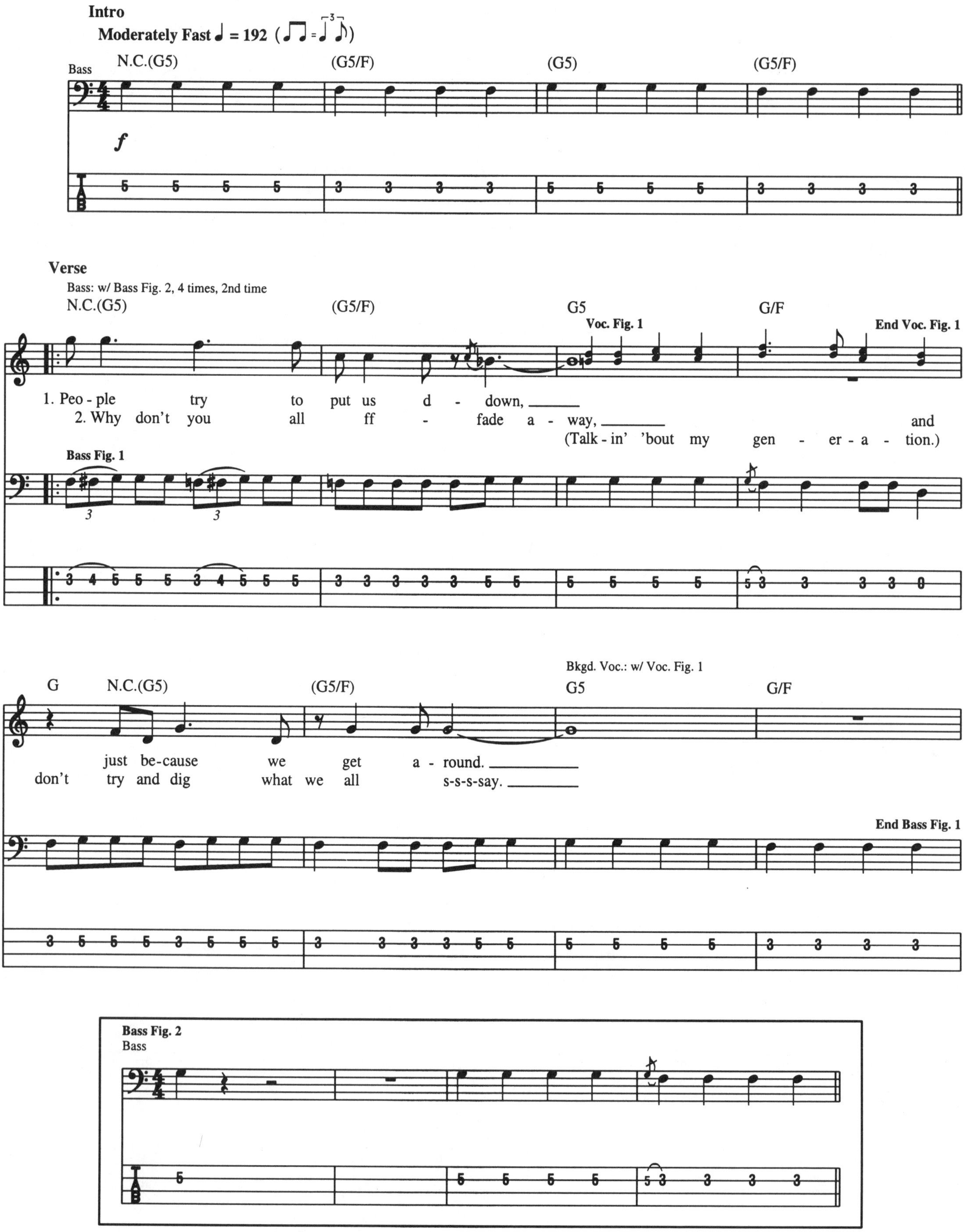

Bass: w/ Bass Fig. 1, 1st time, simile
N.C.(G5)
(G5/F)
Bkgd. Voc.: w/ Voc. Fig. 1
G5
G/F
Things they do look aw - ful c - c - - cold. I
not try - in' to cause a big s - s - sen - sa - tion, I'm just
G5 N.C.(G5)
(G/F)
G5
G/F
hope I die be - fore I get old.
talk - in' 'bout my g - g - g - gen-er-a - tion.
Yeah, my gen - er - a -
Chorus
1.
G
Gsus4
G7
Gsus4
G
Gsus4
G7
Gsus4
- tion.
Said my gen - er - a - tion, ba - by.
Bass
2.
G7
Gsus4
G
Gsus4
G7
Gsus4
Bass Solo
G5 N.C.
My gen - er - a - tion, ba - by.
full
G5
G6
G7
G6
G5
N.C.
1/4
1/4
G5
G6
G7
G6
G5
N.C.
full

G5 G6 G7 G6 G5 N.C.
G6 G7 G6 G Gsus4 G7 Gsus4 G Gsus4
Verse
G7 Gsus4 A N.C. A A/G
Voc. Fig. 2
End Voc. Fig. 2
3. Why don't you all ff fade a - way. Yeah,
(Talk - in' 'bout my gen - er - a - tion.)
Bass Fig. 3
End Bass Fig. 3
Bass: w/ Bass Fig. 3, 3 times
Bkgd. Voc.: w/ Voc. Fig. 2
A N.C. A A/G
don't try and d - dig what we all s - s - s - s - s - say.
Bkgd. Voc.: w/ Voc. Fig. 2
A N.C. A A/G
Not try - in' to cause big sen - sa - tion, just
Bkgd. Voc.: w/ Voc. Fig. 2
A N.C. A A/G
talk - in' 'bout my g - gen - er - a - tion. Ba - by, my gen - er - a -

Chorus
A Asus4 A Asus4
tion, this is my gen-er-a - tion, ba - by.
Bass
A Asus4 A Asus4 A Asus4 Bb5
My, my, ge - gen - er - a-tion. My, my, ooh, my, my. (1st time) My, my,
Verse
Bb5/Ab Bb5 N.C. Bb5 Bb6 Bb7 Bb6
Voc. Fig. 3
End Voc. Fig. 3
my, gen-er-a-tion. 4. Peo-ple try to put us d-down
(Talk-in' 'bout my gen - er-a-tion.)
Bass Fig. 4
End Bass Fig. 4
Bass: w/ Bass Fig. 4
Bkgd. Voc.: w/ Voc. Fig. 3
Bb5 N.C. (Bb) (Bb/Ab) Ab5
just be-cause we g - g - g - get a - round.
Bass: w/ Bass Fill 1
Bkgd. Voc.: w/ Voc. Fig. 3
Bass: w/ Bass Fig. 4, last 3 meas.
Bkgd. Voc.: w/ Voc. Fig. 3
Bb5 N.C. Bb Bbsus4 Bb Bbsus4
Things they do look aw - ful c - c - cold, yeah, I
Bass Fill 1
Bass

Bass: w/ Bass Fig. 4
Bkgd. Voc.: w/ Voc. Fig. 3
B♭ N.C.
B♭
B♭sus4
hope I die be - fore I get old.
My gen - er -
Chorus
B♭
B♭sus4
B♭
B♭sus4
a - tion.
This is my gen - er - a - tion, ba - by.
Mm
Bass
B♭
B♭sus4
B♭
B♭sus4
my, my, my, my, my gen - er - a - tion, gen - er - a - tion.
Guitar Solo
C5
F/C
C
F/C
C
F/C
C
F/C
C
F/C

C
Bb/C
C
Bb/C
C
Bb/C
C
Bb/C
Outro
w/ Lead Voc. ad lib.
C
Talk - in' 'bout my gen - er - a - tion. Talk - in' 'bout my gen - er - a - tion.
Talk - in' 'bout my gen - er - a - tion. Talk - in' 'bout my gen - er - a - tion.
C
play 4 times
C
Talk - in' 'bout my gen - er - a - tion.

One Thing Leads to Another

Words and Music by Cy Curnin, Jamie West-Oram, Adam Woods, Rupert Greenall and Alfred Agius

Abmaj7 Ab5 Abmaj7 Bbm7
(no3rd) (no3rd)
Ab5
ir - ri - tates. Com - mun - i - cate, pull out your par - ty piece. You see di - men - sions in
Abmaj7 Ab5 Abmaj7 Bbm7
(no3rd) (no3rd)
two, state your case with black or white. But when one
Ab5 Abmaj7 Ab5 Abmaj7 Bbm7
(no3rd) (no3rd)
lit - tle cross leads to shots, grit your teeth. You run for cov - er so dis -
Chorus
Bkgd. Voc.: w/ Voc. Fig. 1
Bbm7 Ab5 Abmaj7 Ab5 Abmaj7 Bbm7
(no3rd) (no3rd)
creet. Why don't they do what they say? Say what you mean. Oh ba - by,
Bass Fig. 2
End Bass Fig. 2
w/ Bass Fig. 2 (3 times)
Bkgd. Voc.: w/ Voc. Fig. 1
Ab5
one thing leads to an - oth - er. You told me some-thing wrong. I know I lis - ten too long.
Abmaj7 Ab5 Abmaj7 Bbm7
(no3rd) (no3rd)
But then one thing leads to an - oth - er. 2. The im -
Voc. Fig. 1
(Ah.)

Verse
Bbm7 Ab5 Abmaj7 (no3rd) Ab5 Abmaj7 (no3rd) Bbm7
pres - sion that you sell
pass-es in and out like a scent,
but the long
Ab5 Abmaj7 (no3rd) Ab5 Abmaj7 (no3rd) Bbm7
face that you see
comes from liv - ing close to your fears.
Ab5 Abmaj7 (no3rd) Ab5 Abmaj7 (no3rd) Bbm7
If this is up, then I'm up, but you're run - ning out of sight.
Bkgd. Voc.: w/ Voc. Fig. 2
Ab5
You've seen your name on the walls.
And when one lit - tle bump leads to
Voc. Fig. 2
(One bump. Shock beat oh. Shock. Bump.)

Abmaj7 (no3rd) Ab5 Abmaj7 (no3rd) Bbm7
shock, miss a beat. You run for cov - er, and there's heat. Why don't they do
Chorus
Bkgd. Voc.: w/ Voc. Fig. 1
w/ Bass Fig. 2 (4 times)
Bbm7 Ab5 Abmaj7 (no3rd) Ab5 Abmaj7 (no3rd) Bbm7
what they say, say, what they mean? One thing leads to an - oth -
Bkgd. Voc.: w/ Voc. Fig. 1
Ab5 Abmaj7 (no3rd) Ab5 Abmaj7 (no3rd) Bbm7
er. You told me some-thing wrong. I know I lis - ten too long. But then
Interlude
N.C.
4
one thing leads to an - oth - er, yeah, yeah, yeah.
Voc. Fig. 3
End Voc. Fig. 3
(One thing, leads to an - oth - er.)
(One thing.)
3. But it's eas -
(One leads to an - oth - er.)
Verse
w/ Bass Fig. 2 (6 times)
Bbm7 Ab5 Abmaj7 (no3rd) Ab5 Abmaj7 (no3rd) Bbm7
- y to be - lieve some - bod - y's been ly - ing to me.

Ab5 Abmaj7 (no3rd) Ab5 Abmaj7 (no3rd) Bbm7
But when the wrong word goes in the right ear I
Ab5
know you've been ly - ing to me. It's get - ting rough, off the cuff. I've got to
Abmaj7 (no3rd) Ab5 Abmaj7 (no3rd) Bbm7
say e - nough's e - nough. Big - ger, the hard - er he falls. But when the
Bkgd. Voc.: w/ Voc. Fig. 2
Ab5 Abmaj7 (no3rd) Ab Abmaj7 (no3rd) Bm7
wrong an - ti - dote is like a bulge in the throat, you run for cov - er in the
Chorus
Bkgd. Voc.: w/ Voc. Fig. 1 (2 times)
w/ Bass Fig. 2 (4 times)
Bbm7 Ab5 Abmaj7 (no3rd) Ab5 Abmaj7 (no3rd) Bbm7
heat. Why don't they do what they say, say, what they mean?
Ab5
One thing leads to an - oth - er. You told me some-thing wrong. I know I lis - ten too long.
Abmaj7 (no3rd) Ab5 Abmaj7 (no3rd) Bbm7
But then one thing leads to an - oth - er, yeah, yeah.

Outro

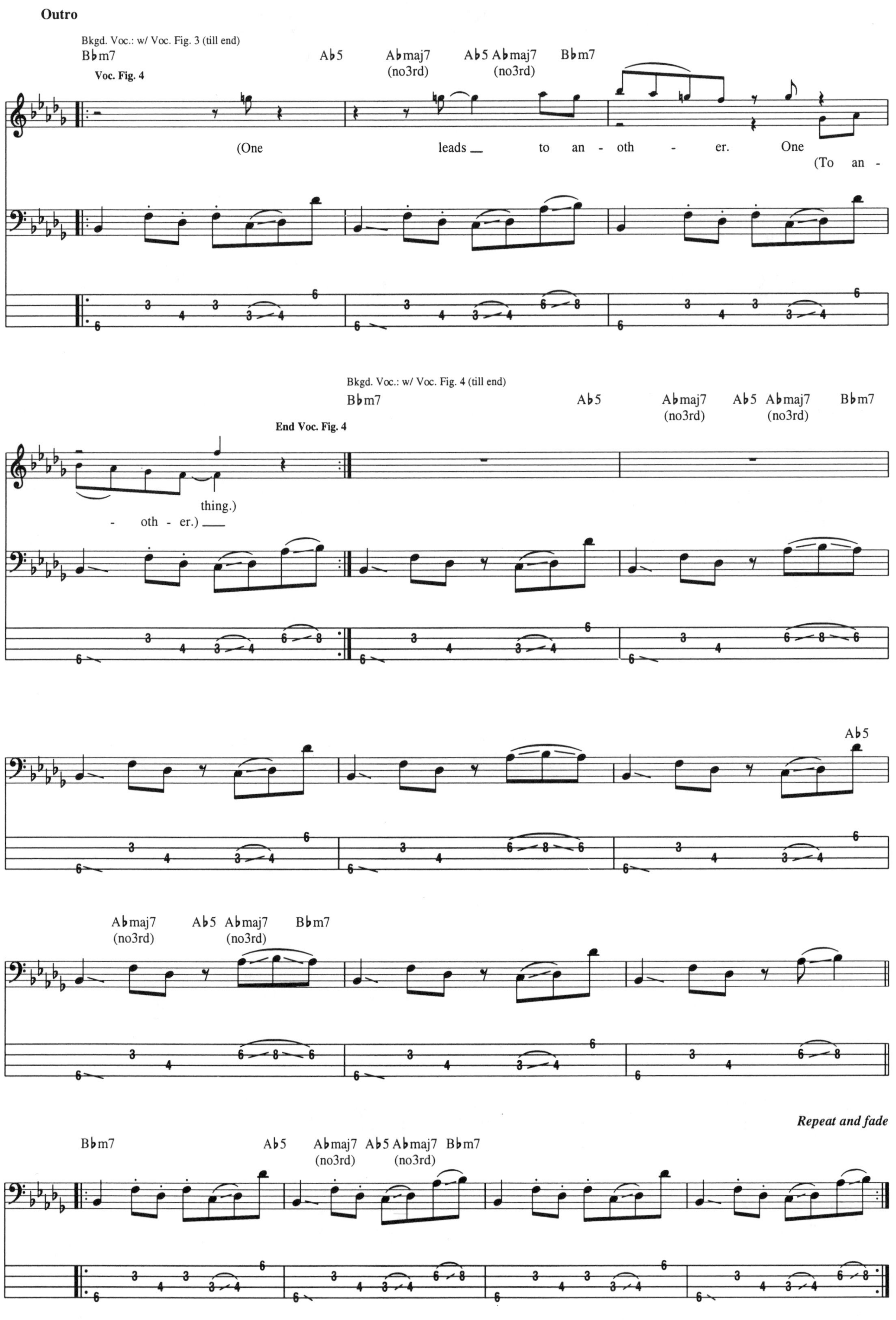
Bkgd. Voc.: w/ Voc. Fig. 3 (till end)
Bbm7
Voc. Fig. 4
Ab5
Abmaj7 (no3rd)
Ab5 Abmaj7 (no3rd)
Bbm7
(One leads to an - oth - er. One
(To an -
Bkgd. Voc.: w/ Voc. Fig. 4 (till end)
Bbm7
End Voc. Fig. 4
Ab5
Abmaj7 (no3rd)
Ab5 Abmaj7 (no3rd)
Bbm7
thing.)
- oth - er.)
Ab5
Abmaj7 (no3rd)
Ab5 Abmaj7 (no3rd)
Bbm7
Repeat and fade
Bbm7
Ab5
Abmaj7 (no3rd)
Ab5 Abmaj7 (no3rd)
Bbm7

Same Old Song & Dance

Words and Music by Steven Tyler and Joe Perry

Intro
Moderate Rock ♩ = 120
* E7(no 3rd)
8va
Ah ha,
f
(7)
* Chord symbols reflect basic harmony.
8va
right!
1/4
1/4
1/4
Verse
E5
loco
1. Get your - self cool - er, lay your - self low. Co -
1/4

in - ci - den - tal mur - der with noth - in' to show. When the judge - 's con - sti - pa - tion
goes to his head, and his wife's ag - gra - va - tion, you soon end up dead. It's the same
Chorus
G A C5 D5 E5
old sto - ry, same old song and dance, my friend.
G A C5 D5
It's the same old sto - ry, same old song and dance,
1/4
1/4

Verse
E5
my friend.
2. Shady lookin loser you
down and dirty from
1/4
played with my gun. No smooth face lawyer can get you undone.
walk-in' the street with your old hurdy gurdy, no one to meet.
Say love
ain't the same on the south side o' town. You could look but you ain't gonna
Chorus
G A C5 D5
find it around. It's the same old story, same old song and dance.

E5
G
A
C5
my friend. It's the same old sto - ry, same
1/4
1/4
To Coda
D5
F5
G5
A5
C5
D5
old sto - ry, same old song and dance.
Guitar Solo
E5
1/4
Bridge
B5
A5
G5
1. Fate comes a-knock-in', doors start lock-in'. Your old time con-nec-tion, change
2. Saxophone solo

A5 G5 A5 B5 A5 G5 A5 B5 A5 G5 A5 B5
your di - rec - tion. You ain't gon - na change it, can't re - ar - range it. Can't
A5 G5 A5 B5 C#5 D5 D#5 E5
1.
stand the pain when it's all the same to you my friend.
2.
E5
D.S. al Coda
When you're low
Coda
E5

School's Out

Words and Music by Alice Cooper, Neal Smith, Michael Bruce, Glen Buxton and Dennis Dunaway

E5 A/E Em E5 A/E E5 Em7 E5 A/E Em E5 A/E E5 Em7
mak-in' all their noise, 'cause they found new toys.
Pre-Chorus
E5 A/E Em C5 D5 Eb5
Well, we can't sa-lute ya, can't find a flag. If that don't suit ya,
Chorus
G5 Bb5 C5 F5 G5
that's a drag. School's out for sum-mer!
F5 G5 Bb5 C5 F5 G5 F5 G5
School's out for ev-er
Bass Fig. 1
End Bass Fig. 1

w/ Bass Fig. 1
B♭5 C5 F5 G5 F5 G5
School's been blown to piec - es!
Bridge
C Csus2♯11 C Csus2♯11 C Csus2♯11 C Csus2♯11
No more pen - cils, no more books,
Dsus4/2 D D9 D Dsus4/2 D
no more teach - er's dir - ty looks. Yeah!
(No more teach - er's dir - ty looks.)
Guitar Solo
E5 A/E N.C. Em E5 A/E Em E5 A/E E5 Em E5 A/E Em
Play 3 times
2. Well, we got

Verse
E5 A/E E5 Em7 E5 A/E Em E5 A/E E5 Em7 E5 A/E Em
— no class, — and we got — no prin - ci - ples, — and we got —
sim.
E5 A/E E5 Em7 E5 A/E Em E5 A/E E5 Em7 E5 A/E Em
— no in - no - cence. We can't e - ven think of a word that rhymes! —
Chorus
w/ Bass Fig. 1 (2 times)
G5 Bb5 C5 F5 G5 F5 G5 Bb5 C5 F5 G5 F5 G5
School's out for sum - mer! School's out for ev - er! My
G5 F C/G
school's been blown to piec - es!
Bridge
C Csus2#11 C Csus2#11
No more pen - cils,
w/ children's laughter & talking
C Csus2#11 C Csus2#11 Dsus 2/4 D D9 D Dsus 2/4 D
no more books, — no more teach - er's dir - ty

D9 D C Csus2#11 C Csus2#11 C Csus2#11 C Csus2#11
looks Out for sum - mer, out til fall.
Dsus2/4 D D9 D Dsus2/4 D N.C.
We might not go back at all!
Chorus
w/ Bass Fig. 1 (3 times)
G5 Bb5 C5 F5 G5 F5 G5 G5 Bb5 C5
School's out for ev - er! School's out for
F5 G5 F5 G5 Bb5 C5 F5 G5 F5 G5
sum-mer! School's out with fe-ver!
w/ school bell
w/ children's cheers & tape effects
Gm F C
School's out com - plete - ly!

Sir Duke

Words and Music by Stevie Wonder

Pre-Chorus
F♯ E9 E♭9 D9 D♭9 D9 E♭9 E9
But just be-cause a rec-ord has a groove don't make it in the groove. But you can
now. For there's Ba-sie, Mil-ler, Satch-mo and the king of all, Sir Duke. And with a
2 X 4 4 3 X 5 3 2 2 1 1 0 0 4 4 0 0 1 1 2 (2) 14
To Coda Chorus
E♭9 D9 D♭9 D9 E♭9 E9 F9 F♯9
tell right a-way at let-ter A when the peo-ple start to move. They can feel it all
voice like El-la's ring-ing out there's no way the band could lose.
2 2 1 1 0 0 4 4 0 1 2 3 4 2 4 X 4 X 4 2
Fm Emaj7 D♯m C♯m F♯
o - - ver. They can feel it all o - ver peo - ple.
3 X 6 5 X 6 3 2 4 X 2 X 2 1 4 4 4 2 3 4 4 X 4 3
B Fm Emaj7 D♯m
They can feel it all o - ver. They can feel it all
2 4 X 4 X 4 2 3 6 X 5 X 6 3 2 4 X 2 X 2 1

Interlude
C♯m
F♯
N.C.
o - ver ___ peo - ple, go!
Bass Fig. 1
D.S. al Coda
End Bass Fig. 1
Coda
Chorus
4th time, w/ Bass Fill 3
B
Fm
2nd, 3rd & 4th times, w/ Bass Fill 2
Emaj7
D♯m
You can feel it all ___ o - ver. ___
You can feel it all ___
Bass Fill 1
End Bass Fill 1
Bass Fill 2
Bass Fill 3

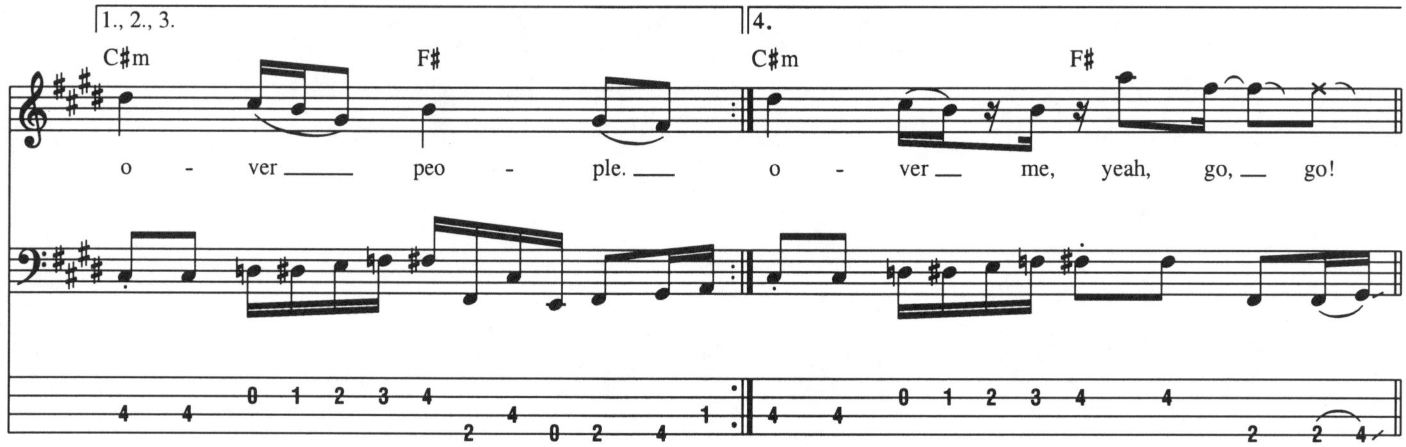

Interlude

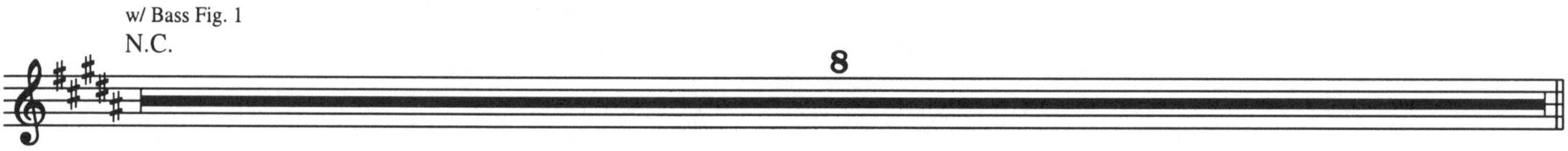

Chorus

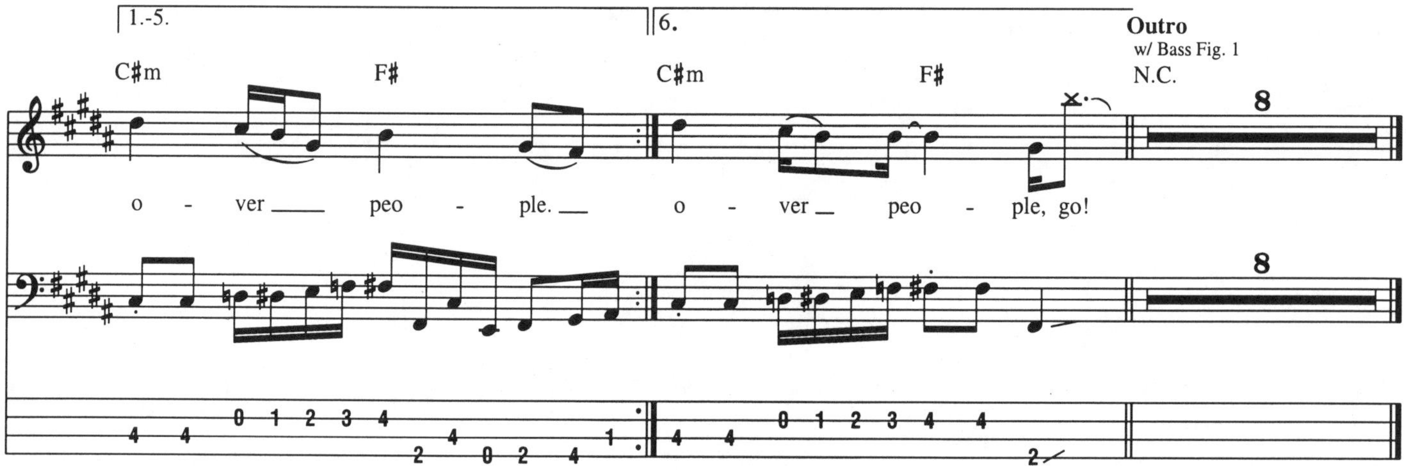

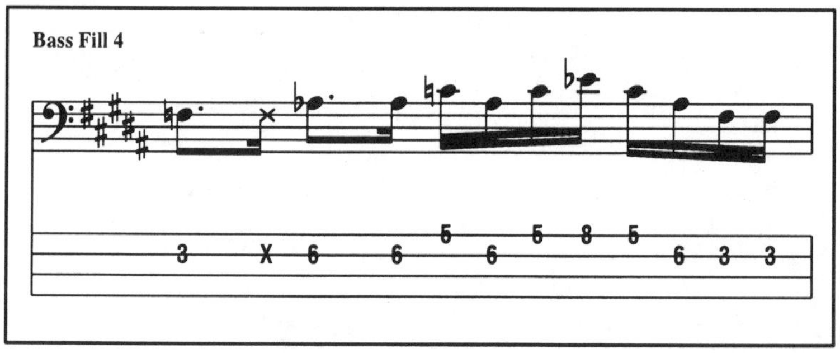

Smoke on the Water

Words and Music by Ritchie Blackmore, Ian Gillan, Roger Glover, Jon Lord and Ian Paice

F5
mo - bile,
we did - n't have much time.
F5
But Frank Zap - pa and the Moth - ers
were at the best place a - round.
G5
But some stu - pid with a flare gun
Chorus
F5
G5
C5
A♭5
burned the place to the ground.
Smoke on the wa - ter,
Bass Fig. 1

G5
C5
Ab5
a fire in the sky.
Smoke on the wa - ter.
End Bass Fig. 1
G5 Bb5 C5 G5 Bb5 Db5 C5 G5 Bb5 C5 Bb5 G5
1.
2.
Verse
G5
2. They burned down the gam - bling house, it
F5
died with an aw-ful sound.
A Funk-y Claude was run-ning in and out,

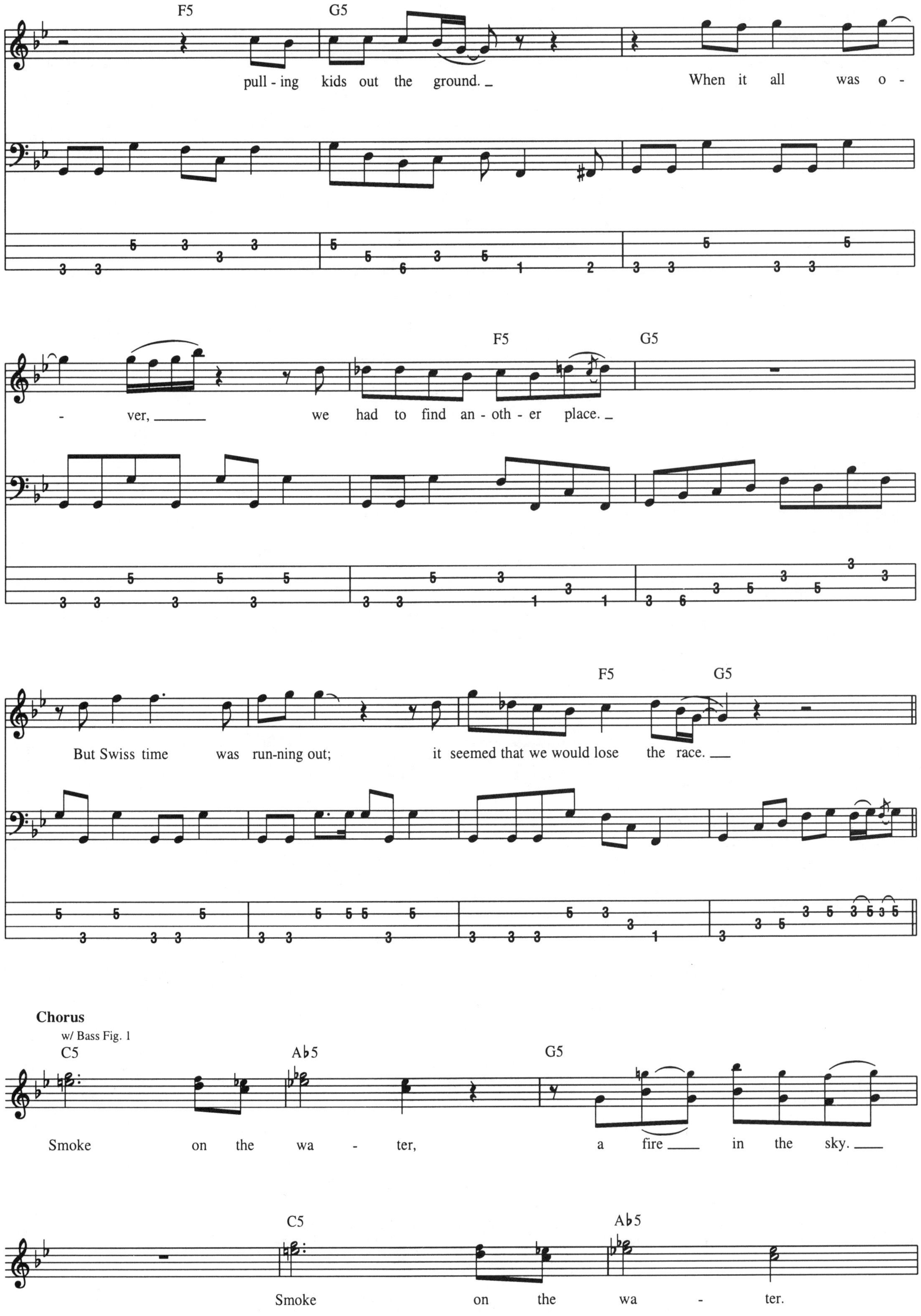
F5
G5
pull - ing kids out the ground.
When it all was o -
ver,
we had to find an - oth - er place.
But Swiss time was run-ning out;
it seemed that we would lose the race.
Chorus
w/ Bass Fig. 1
C5
Ab5
Smoke on the wa - ter,
a fire in the sky.
Smoke on the wa - ter.

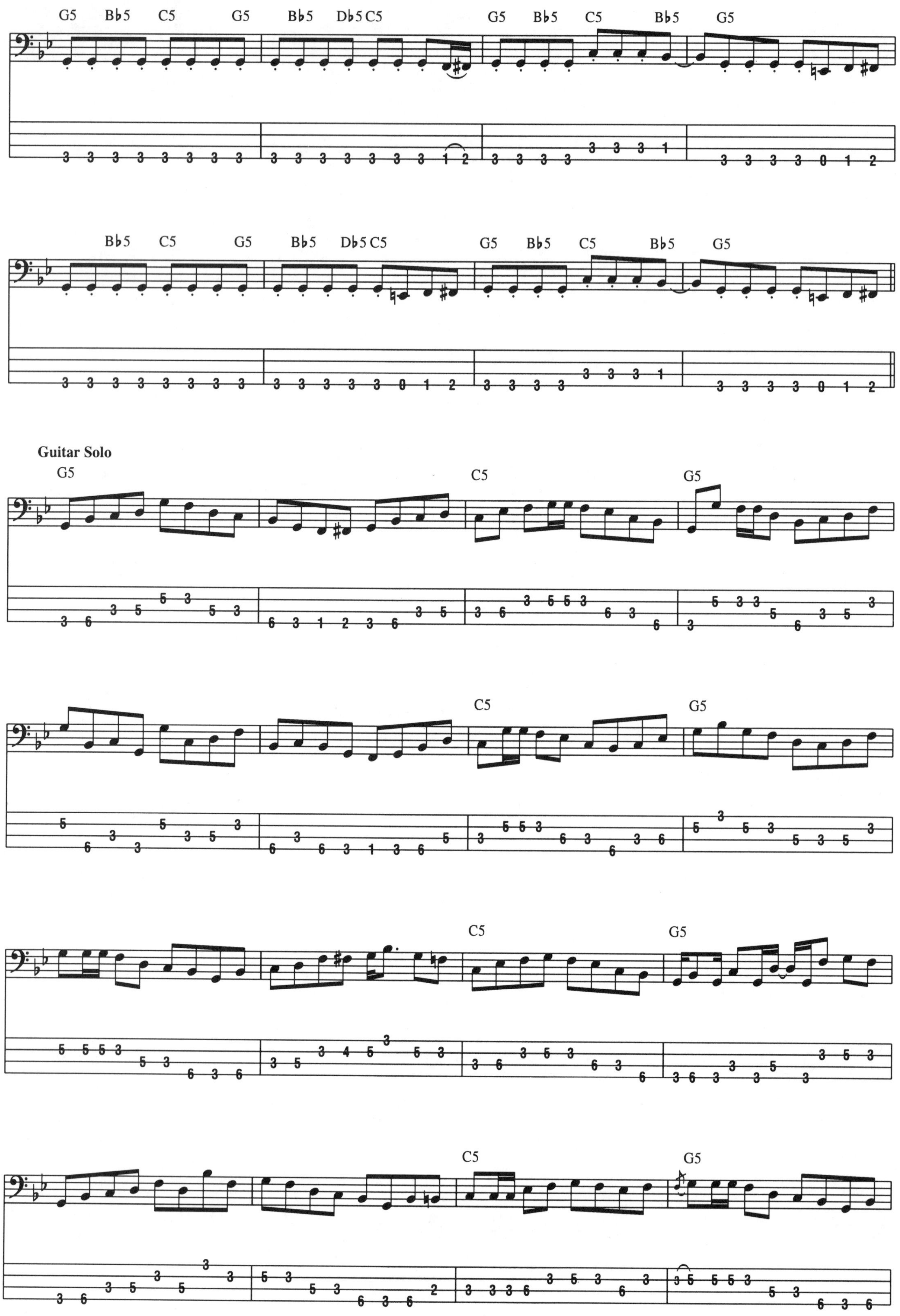
G5 Bb5 C5 G5 Bb5 Db5 C5 G5 Bb5 C5 Bb5 G5
Bb5 C5 G5 Bb5 Db5 C5 G5 Bb5 C5 Bb5 G5
Guitar Solo
G5 C5 G5
C5 G5
C5 G5
C5 G5

C5
F5
G5
Bb5
C5
G5
Bb5
Db5 C5
G5
Bb5
C5
Bb5
G5
Bb5
C5
G5
Bb5
Db5 C5
G5
Bb5
C5
G5
Verse
G5
3. We end - ed up at the Grand
F5
G5
Ho - tel,
it was emp - ty,
cold and bare.
But with the

F5
Roll - ing truck Stones thing just out - side, make - ing our
G5
mu - sic there. With a few red lights, a few old beds
F5
G5
we made a place to sweat. No mat - ter what we
F5
G5
get out of this, I know, I know we'll nev - er for - get.

Chorus
w/ Bass Fig. 1
C5 Ab5 G5
Smoke on the wa - ter, a fire in the sky.
C5 Ab5
Smoke on the wa - ter.
G5 Bb5 C5 G5 Bb5 Db5 C5 G5 Bb5 C5 Bb5 G5
1.
2.
G5 G5 Bb5 C5 G5 Bb5 Db5 C5
G5 Bb5 C5 Bb5 G5 G5
Outro-Organ Solo
Repeat and fade
G5 Bb5 C5 G5 Bb5 Db5 C5 G5 Bb5 C5 Bb5 G5

Spirits in the Material World

Written and Composed by Sting

Am G Em Am G Em
There is no blood - y rev - o - lu - tion.
but it's the rhet - o - ric of fail-ure.
We
Chorus
Dm G Em Dm G Em Dm
are spir-its in the ma-te - rial world, are spir-its in the ma-te - rial world,
G Em Dm G Em Dm
are spir-its in the ma-te - rial world, are spir-its in the ma-te - rial world.
1.
2.
G Em Dm Em F G F/A G
in the ma - te - rial world.

F Em Dm Am G Em Am G
2nd time
Em Am G Em Am G
Where does the an - swer lie
Em Am G Em Am G
liv- ing from day to day?
Em Am G Em Am G
If it's some - thing we can't buy,
D.S. al Coda, Repeat Chorus, and Fade
Em Am G Em Am G Em
there must be an - oth - er way.
We -

Suffragette City

Words and Music by David Bowie

D F G
straight-en my face, this mel-low thighed chick just put my spine out of place.
End Bass Fig. 1
w/ Bass Fig. 1
A F G A
(Hey, man!) My school day's in - sane. (Hey, man!) My
F G A B D
work's down the drain. (Hey, man!) Uh, she's a tot - al blam blam, she
F G
said she had to squeeze it but she… an' then she… Ah, don't
Chorus
A D F
lean on me, man, 'cause you can't af - ford the tick-et back from Suf - fra-gette Cit -
G A D
y! Uh, don't lean on me, man, 'cause you ain't got time to check it.

To Coda
F C G G#5 A5 G
You know my Suf-fra-gette Cit - y is out-ta sight! She's al -
A
right! Hmm.
Verse
w/ Bass Fig. 1
A F G A F G
2. (Hey, Man!) Ah, Hen-ry, don't be un - kind, go 'way! (Hey, man!) I can't take you this time, no way.
D.S. al Coda
A B D F G
(Hey, man!) Di-droog-ie, don't crash here. There's on - ly room for one an' here she comes, here she comes! Ah, don't
Coda
Guitar Solo
A F G A
right! Oh, hit me!

F G A B
Chorus
F G A D
Uh, don't _ lean on me, man, 'cause you can't af - ford the tick - et
F C G A
back from Suf - fra - gette Cit - y! Uh, don't _ lean on me, man, 'cause you
D F C G G#5 A5
ain't got time to check it. You know my Suf - fra - gette Cit - y! Don't _

A D F C
lean on me, man, 'cause you can't af - ford the tick - et back from Suf - fra - gette Cit -
G A D
y! Uh, don't lean on me, man, 'cause you ain't got time to check it.
F C G G#5 A5
You know my Suf - fra - gette Cit - y is out - ta sight!
Outro
G A F G
Wa! she's al - right! My suf - fra - gette Cit -

A
F
G
A
y!
My Suf - fra - gette Cit - y!
F
G
A
F
G
I'm back from Suf - fra - gette Cit - y!
I'm back from Suf - fra - gette Cit -
A
F
G
A
y!
Hoo ho!
My Suf - fra - gette Cit - y!
Hoo
F
G
A
F
G
ho!
Suf - fra - gette Cit - y!
Hoo ha!
My Suf - fra - gette Cit -

A
F
E
y!
Hoo _ ha!
my Suf-fra-gette…
6/7 7 7 7 7 7 7 3
3 3 3 3 3 3 2
2 2 2 2 2 2 2 2
2 2 2 2 2 2 2 2
A
N.C.
A
F
Ah,
wham bam, thank you, ma'am!
cresc.
2 2 2 2 2 2 2 0
2
7 7 7 7 7 7 7 7
A
F
My Suf - fra - gette Cit - y!
My Suf - fra - gette Cit -
(Oo,
yeah,
oo!
3 3 3 3 3 3 5 5
7 7 7 7 7 7 7 7
3 3 3 3 3 3 5 5
A
F
A
F
y!
Quite al - right!
My Suf - fra - gette Cit - y!
Too
fine!
Oo!)
7 7 7 7 7 7 7 7 3
3 3 3 3 3 3 5 5
7 7 7 7 7 7 7 7 3

A F
Uh, Suf - fra - gette Cit - y!
(Oo, oo!
Oh, my Suf - fra - gette Cit -
A F A F
y! Yeah!
Oo, hoo, hoo!
Ho! My Suf - fra - gette Cit - y! Ah! Woo!
Oo, oo!
A F
My Suf - fra - gette Cit - y!
Oo, oo!)
Ah, Suf - fra- gette...
E A
Suf - fra - gette!
cresc.

Susie-Q

Words and Music by Dale Hawkins, Stan Lewis and Eleanor Broadwater

A
C
B
3rd time, w/ Bass Fill 1
E7
ba - by, I love you, Su - sie - Q.
and nev - er leave me blue, Su - sie - Q.
3rd time, w/ Bass Fill 3
Like the way you walk. I like the way you talk.
Well, say that you'll be mine. Well, say that you'll be mine.
3rd time, w/ Bass Fill 2
A
I like the way you walk, I like the way you talk,
Well, say that you'll be mine, ba - by, all the time,
C
B
E7
To Coda 2
To Coda 1
Su - sie - Q.
Su - sie - Q.
Bass Fill 1
End Bass Fill 1

Guitar Solo
E
Bass Fill 2
End Bass Fill 2
A
C
B
E
A
C
B
E
Interlude
E7
1., 2., 3.
4.
D.S. al Coda 1
2. Well, say that you'll be true.

Coda 1
Guitar Solo
E
1., 2., 3.
4.
Em
E
Oo,
oo,
Bass Fill 3
End Bass Fill 3
oo.
Interlude
E7

D.S. al Coda 2
3. Oh, Su - sie - Q.
Coda 2
Verse
E7
4. Oh, Su - sie - Q.
Oh, Su - sie - Q.
A
Oh, Su - sie - Q, ba - by, I love you,
C
B
E7
Su - sie - Q.

Outro-Solo

Sweet Child O' Mine

Words and Music by W. Axl Rose, Slash, Izzy Stradlin', Duff McKagan and Steven Adler

2nd time, w/ Bass Fill 1
2nd time, w/ Bass Fill 2
G
mem - o - ries, where ev - 'ry thing was as fresh as the bright blue sky.
rain. I'd hate to look in to those eyes and
D
Now and then when I see her face she
see an ounce of pain. Her hair re - minds me of a warm safe place where
Cadd9
G
takes me a - way to that spe - cial place, and if I stared too long, I'll
as a child I'd hide, and pray for the thun - der
Bass Fill 1
Bass Fill 2

2nd time, w/ Bass Fill 3
D
prob - 'ly break down and cry.
and the rain to qui - et - ly pass me. by.
Chorus
2nd time, w/ Bass Fill 4
3rd time, w/ Bass Fill 5
A5
B5
C5
D
Whoa, whoa, whoa, sweet child o' mine.
1.
To Coda
A5
B5
C5
D
Whoa, oh, oh, oh, sweet love o' mine.

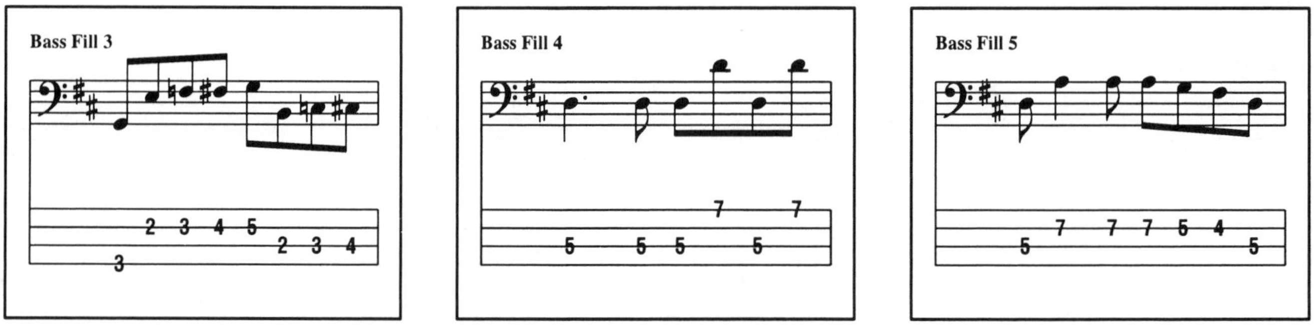
Bass Fill 3
Bass Fill 4
Bass Fill 5

Interlude
D
C
G
D
2.
D
Interlude
D
C
G
D
C
D.S. al Coda
G
D

Coda
D
A5
B5
Oh, oh, oh, oh,
C5
D
sweet child o' mine.
Woo yeah, yeah!
A5
B5
C5
D5
D♯5
Ooh, sweet love o' mine.
1., 2., 3.
4.
Guitar Solo
Em
C
B7
Am
A5
Em
G5
A5
B5
C5
D5
G5
Play 4 times

Outro

E5 G5 A5 C5 D5 G5
Where do we go? — Where do we go — now? Where do we go. —
E5 G5 A5 C5 D5 G5
Where do we go? — Whispered: Sweet Child! Where do we go — now?
E5 G5 A5 C5 D5 G5
I, I, I, I, I, I I, I. Where do we go — now, now. —
E5 G5 A5 B5 C5 D5 G5
Where do we go. — Ah. — Where do we go — now?

E5 G5 A5 B5
Where do we go? Where do we go now?
C5 D5 G5 E5 G5 A5 B5
Where do we go? Where do we go now?
E5 D5 B5 B♭5 A5 G5 E5 G5 A5
No, no, no, no, no, no, no. Sweet child, sweet child
C5 D5 E5
o' mine.

Sweet Emotion

Words and Music by Steven Tyler and Tom Hamilton

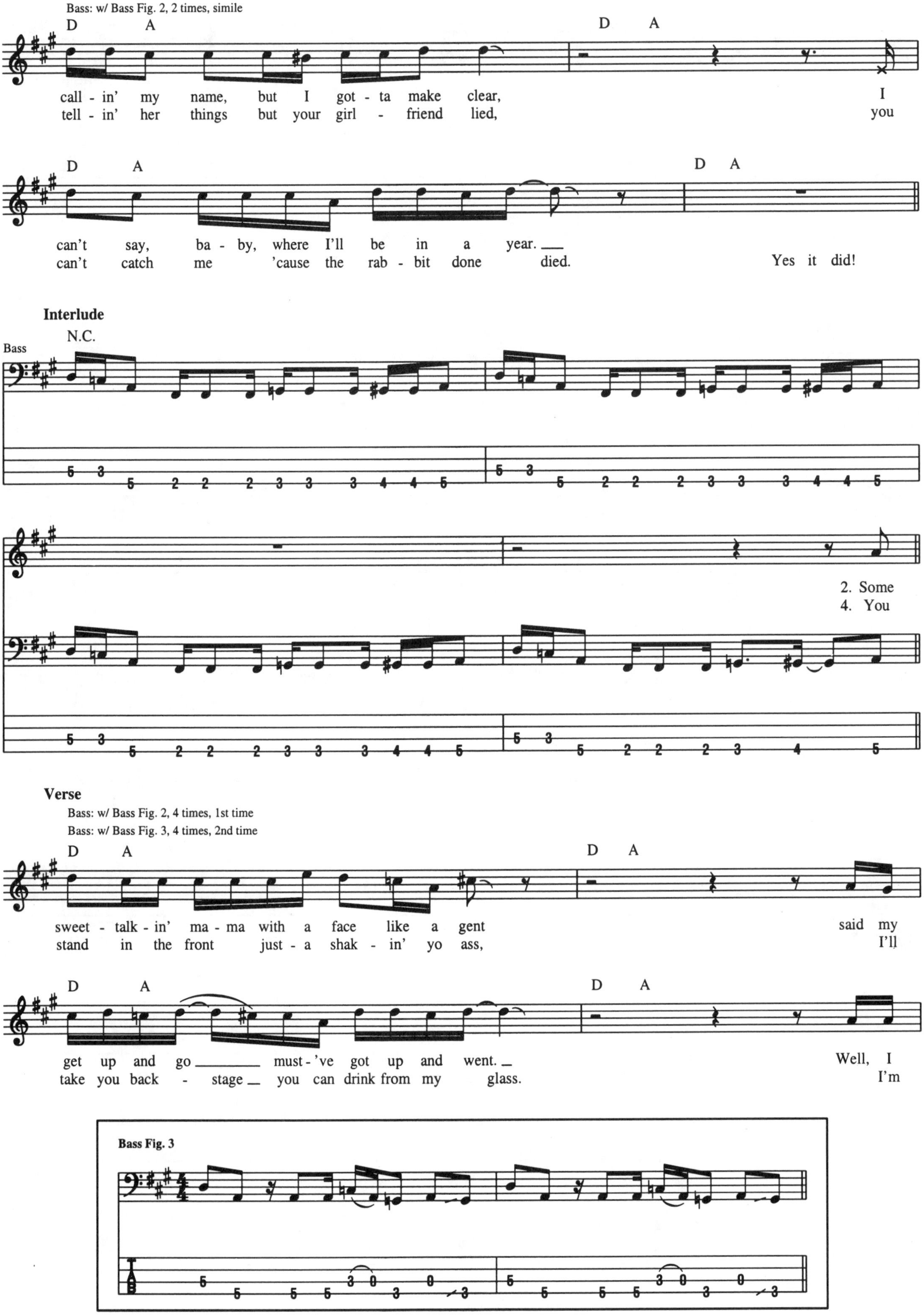

Bass: w/ Bass Fig. 2, 2 times, simile
D A D A
call - in' my name, but I got - ta make clear, I
tell - in' her things but your girl - friend lied, you
D A D A
can't say, ba - by, where I'll be in a year.
can't catch me 'cause the rab - bit done died. Yes it did!
Interlude
N.C.
Bass
2. Some
4. You
Verse
Bass: w/ Bass Fig. 2, 4 times, 1st time
Bass: w/ Bass Fig. 3, 4 times, 2nd time
D A D A
sweet - talk - in' ma - ma with a face like a gent said my
stand in the front just - a shak - in' yo ass, I'll
D A D A
get up and go must - 've got up and went. Well, I
take you back - stage you can drink from my glass. I'm
Bass Fig. 3

D A
got good news, she's a real ___ good li - ar,
talk-in' bout some - thin' you can sure un - der - stand,
D A
'cause my
'cause a
D A
back - stage boo - gie set yo' pants on fire.
month on the road and I'll be eat - in' from your hand.
D A
Interlude
N.C.
Bass
To Coda
Chorus
Bass: w/ Bass Fig. 1, 4 times, simile
N.C.(A)
(D/A)
1.
(A)
2.
(A)
D.S. al Coda
Sweet ___ e - mo - tion
tion.
3. I
Coda
Outro
Play 12 Times and Fade

Takin' Care of Business

Words and Music by Randy Bachman

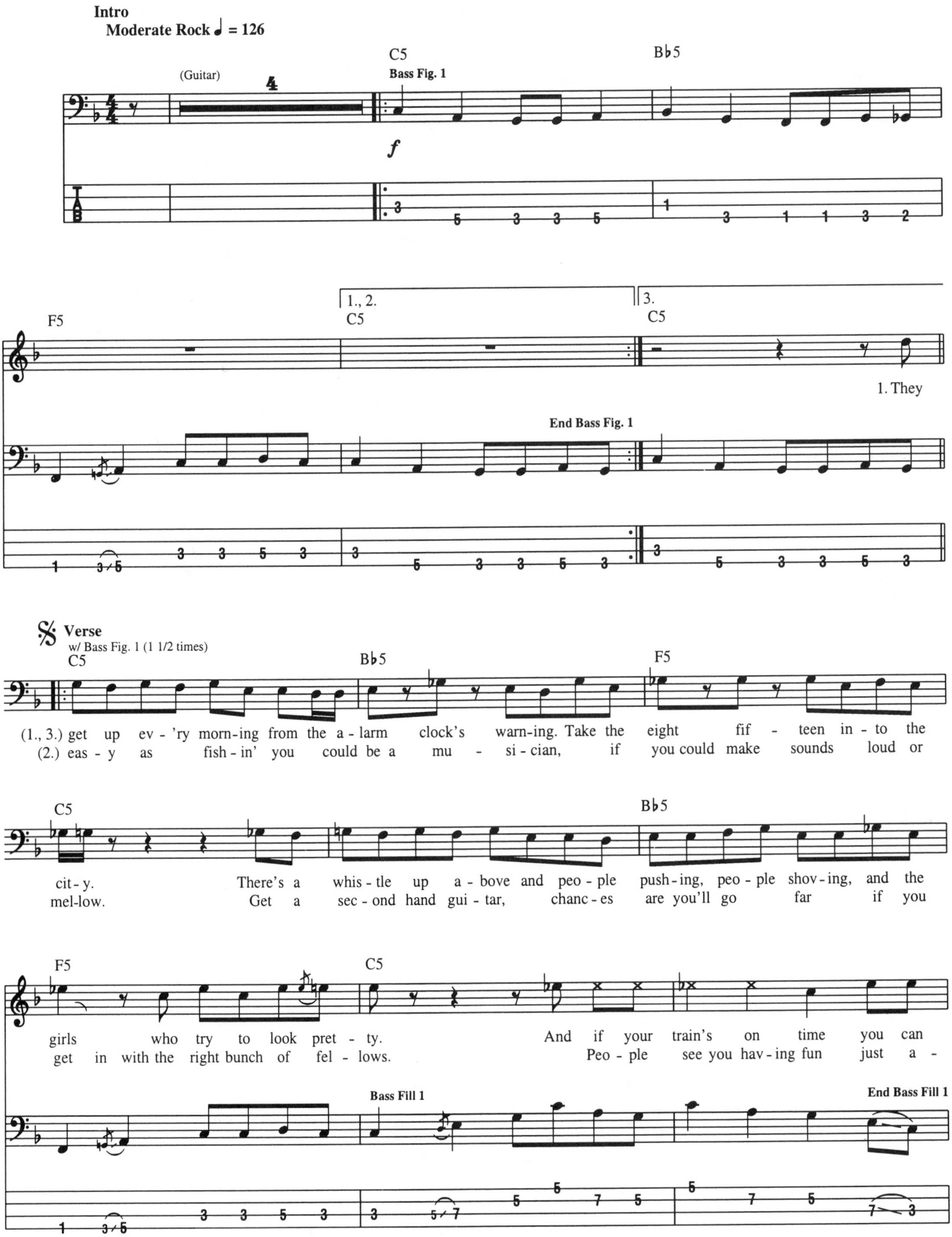

w/ Bass Fig. 1 (last 3 meas.)
Bb5
F5
C5
get to work by nine and start your slav - ing jobs to get your pay. __ If you
ly - ing in the sun. Tell them that you like it this way. ___ It's the
w/ Bass Fig. 1
Bb5
F5
ev - er get an - noyed, look at me, I'm self em-ployed. I love to work at noth - ing all day. _
work that we a - void and we're all self em-ployed. We love to work at noth - ing all day. _
Chorus
w/ Bass Fig. 1 (2 times)
3rd time, w/ Bass Fig. 1 (1st 3 meas.)
C5
C5
Bb5
And I've been tak - ing care of busi - ness ev - 'ry day. __ Tak -
And we've been tak - ing care of busi - ness ev - 'ry day. __ Tak -
3rd time, w/ Bass Fill 1
F5
C5
- ing care of busi - ness ev - 'ry way. I've been tak - ing care of busi - ness,
- ing care of busi - ness ev - 'ry way. We've been tak - ing care of busi - ness,
3rd time, w/ Bass Fig. 1 (last 3 meas.)
To Coda
Bb5
F5
C5
it's all mine. _ Tak - ing care of bus - ness and work - ing o - ver - time, work out.
it's all mine. _ Tak - ing care of busi - ness and work - ing o - ver - time.
1.
Interlude
w/ Bass Fig. 1 (1st 3 meas.)
C5
Bb5
F5
w/ Bass Fill 2
C5
w/ Bass Fig. 1 (last 3 meas.)
Bb5
F5
C5
2.
Guitar solo
w/ Bass Fig. 1 (last 3 meas.)
C5
Bb5
2. There's work
F5
w/ Bass Fill 1
C5
w/ Bass Fig. 1 (last 3 meas.)
Bb5
F5
C5
Bass Fill 2
3 5 7 5 5 7 5 3 7 5 5 7 3

Interlude
C5
Bass tacet
N.C.
Bridge
C F Eb
Whoa!_ Al - right. Ow.
Bass Fill 3
End Bass Fill 3
Bb C F Eb Bb C F Eb
Take good care_ of my busi -
Bb C F Eb
ness, when I'm a - way, ev - 'ry day._ Whoa._
Guitar Solo
w/ Bass Fig. 1
C5 Bb5 F5 C5
D.S. al Coda
Bb5 F5 C5
3. They

Coda
Breakdown
Bass: w/ Bass Fill 3
Bass tacet
N.C.
Tak - ing care of busi - ness.
Whoa. Tak - ing care of busi - ness. Tak -
- ing care of busi - ness. Tak - ing care of busi - ness,
C5 N.C. Bb N.C. F
Tak - ing care of busi - ness, ev - 'ry day. Tak -
- ing care of busi - ness, it's all mine. Tak -
N.C. C 1. N.C. C 2.
- ing care of busi - ness ev - 'ry way. Tak - work - ing o - ver - time. Whoa!
- ing care of busi - ness
Outro
w/ Bass Fig. 1 (till end)
*C5 Bb5 F5 C5
Tak - ing care of busi - ness. Tak - ing care of busi - ness. We've been tak -
*tie on repeats
Repeat and fade
Bb5 F5 C5
- ing care of busi - ness. We've been tak - ing care of busi - ness. Tak -

Walk of Life

Words and Music by Mark Knopfler

Verse
A
B7
E
1., 3. Here comes John - ny sing-ing old - ies, gold - ies.
2. Here comes John - ny gon - na tell you the sto - ry.
End Bass Fig. 1
"Be Bop a Lu - La" ba - by, what I say. _ Here comes John - ny sing-ing "I Got - ta Wom - an,"
Hand me down _ my walk - in' shoes. _ Here comes John - ny with the power and the glo - ry.
down in the tun - nel try-in' to make it pay.
Back - beat the talk - in' blues.
He got the ac - tion, he got the mo - tion.
(Ah.
To Coda
Oh, yeah, _ the boy can play. _ De - di - ca - tion, de - vo - tion;
Yeah, the boy can play. Ah.

E
Voc. Fig. 1
B
turn-ing all the night time in - to the day. He do the song a - bout the sweet lov - in' wom - an, he do the
Turn-ing all the night time in - to the day.
E
A
E
B
song a - bout the knife. Well, he do the walk, do the walk of life.
He do the walk, do the walk of
Interlude
A
B7
End Voc. Fig. 1
E
Voc. Fig. 2
End Voc. Fig. 2
A
Yeah! He do the walk of life.
life.)
(Ah.)
B
A
B7
Ooh.
D.S. al Coda
w/ Bass Fig. 1
E
A
B
A
B7
Ooh.

Coda
Bkgd. Voc.: w/ Voc. Fig. 1
E
turn - ing all the night time in - to the day, and af - ter all that vio - lence and
B E A
dou-ble talk, there's just a song in all the trou - ble and the strife. You do the
E B A B7
walk, yeah! You do the walk of life, mm you do the walk of life.
1st time, Bkgd. Voc.: w/ Voc. Fig. 2
w/ Lead Voc. ad lib on repeats
E A
Ooh.
B A B7
Repeat and fade

Walk on the Wild Side

Words and Music by Lou Reed

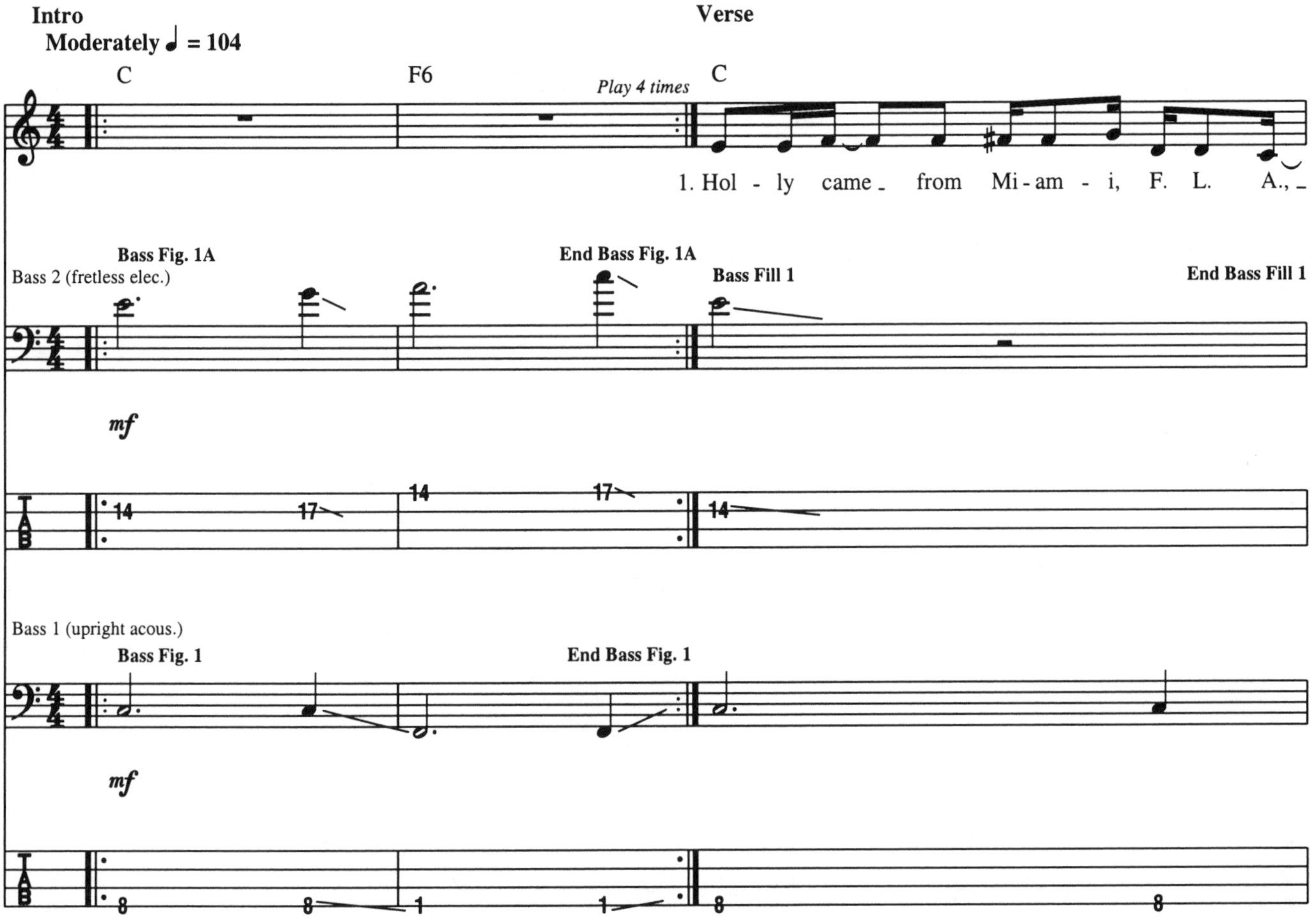

C D F D
Plucked her eye - brows on ___ the way, _ shaved her legs _ and then he was a she. _ She says,
8 10 13 10
Basses 1 & 2: w/ Bass Figs. 1 & 1A (4 times)
C F6 C
"Hey babe, take a walk on the wild _ side." She says, "Hey hon-ey, _ take a walk on the wild _
F6 C F6 C F6
___ side."
Verse
Bass 2: w/ Bass Fill 1
C F6 C
2. Can - dy came _ from out on the is - land, in the back _ room she was ev-'ry-bod - y's
Bass 1
8 10 7 8 5 7 8 10 7 8
F6 C D F D
dar - lin'. But she nev - er lost _ her head, _ e - ven when _ she was giv-in' head. _ She says,
(8) 5 7 8 10 13 10

Bass 2: w/ Bass Fig. 1A (2 times)
C
F6
"Hey babe, take a walk on the wild ___ side." She says,
8 10 9 8 5 6 7
C
F6
"Hey babe, take a walk on the wild side." And the col - ored girls
8 10 9 8 5 6 7
Chorus
Basses 1 & 2: w/ Bass Figs. 1 & 1A (4 times)
C
F6
go... Do, do, do, do, do, do, ___ do, do, do, do, do, do, do, do, ___ do, do.
C
F6
Do, do, do, do, do, do, ___ do, do, do, do, do, do, do, do, ___ do, do.
Bass 1: w/ Bass Fig. 1 (1 1/2 times)
Bass 2: w/ Bass Fig. 1A (2 times)
C
F6
C
F6
C
8
(Do, do, do, do, do, do, _ do, do, do, do, do, do, do, do, _ do, do. Do.)

Verse
Bass 2: w/ Bass Fill 1
F6 C F6
3. Lit-tle Joe nev-er once gave it a-way,
Bass 1
C F6 C D
ev-'ry-bod-y had to pay and pay. A hus-tle here and a hus-tle there,
Bass 2: w/ Bass Fig. 1A (2 times)
F D C
New York Cit-y is the place where they said, "Hey babe, take a walk on the
F6 C F6
wild side." They said, "Hey Joe, take a walk on the wild side."

Bass 1: w/ Bass Fig. 1 (2 times)
C F6 C F6
Bass 2
Verse
Bass 2: w/ Bass Fill 1
C F6 C
4. Su-gar plum fair - ies came and hit the streets
look - ing for soul food and a place to eat.
Bass 1
F6 C D F D
Went to the A-pol - lo, you should have seen them go, go, go. They said,
Bass 2: w/ Bass Fig. 1A (3 1/2 times)
C F6 C
"Hey su-gar, take a walk on the wild side."
They said, "Hey babe, take a walk on the wild

Bass 1: w/ Bass Fig. 1 (2 times)
F6 C F6 C F6
— side." All right? Huh.
Bass 2
Verse
Bass 2: w/ Bass Fill 1
C F6 C
5. Jack - ie is just — speed-in' a - way. — Thought she was James Dean for a day. —
Bass 1
F6 C D F D
Then I guess she had to crash. Val - i - um would-'ve helped that bash. She said,
Bass 2: w/ Bass Fig. 1A (2 times)
C F6
"Hey babe, take a walk on the wild — side." She said,

C
F6
"Hey hon - ey, take a walk on the wild side." And the col-ored girls sing…
Chorus
Bass 1: w/ Bass Fig. 1 (6 times)
Do, do, do, do, do, do, . do, do, do, do, do, do, do, do, - do, do. Do, do, do, do, do, do, . do, do,
Bass 2
do, do, do, do, do, do, - do, do. (Do, do, do, do, do, do, - do, do, do, do, do, do, do, do, - do, do.
(Do, do,do, do,do, do, - do,do, do, do,do, do,do, do, - do, do. (Do, do,do, do,do, do, - do,do,

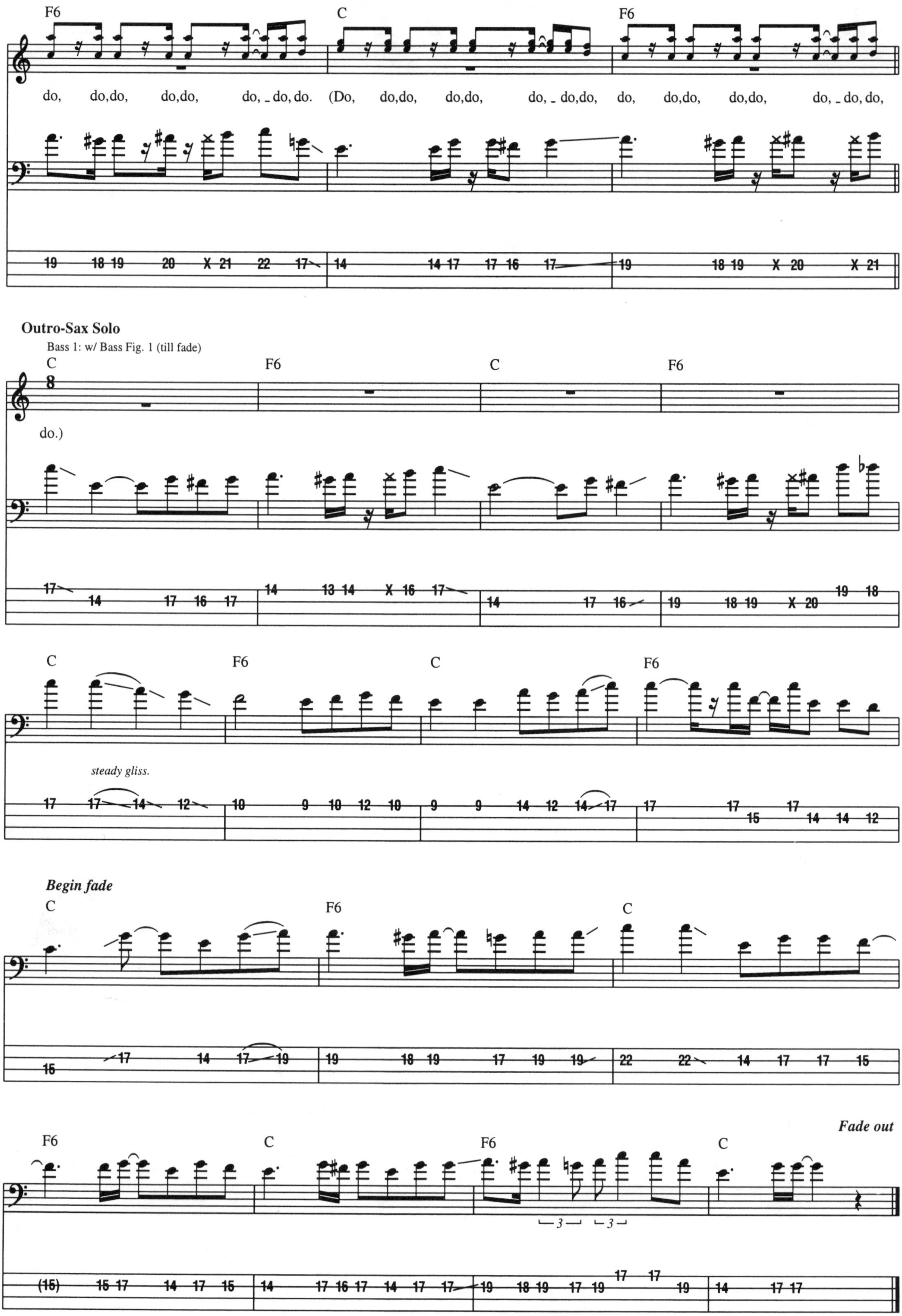
F6
C
F6
do, do,do, do,do, do, _ do, do. (Do, do,do, do,do, do, _ do,do, do, do,do, do,do, do, _ do, do,
Outro-Sax Solo
Bass 1: w/ Bass Fig. 1 (till fade)
C
8
F6
C
F6
do.)
C
F6
C
F6
steady gliss.
Begin fade
C
F6
C
Fade out
F6
C
F6
C

White Room

Words and Music by Jack Bruce and Pete Brown

G/B Bb C D C G/B Bb C
Sil - ver hors - es ran down moon - beams in your
D C G Bb C D C
dark eyes. Dawn - light smiles on you
G/B Bb C D C G Bb
leav - ing, my con - tent - ment. I'll
Bridge
C G Bb
wait in this place where the sun nev - er

A C G
shines; wait in this place where the
B♭ C A
shad - ows run from them - selves.
N.C. D C G/B B♭ C
You said no strings could se - cure you at the
D C G B♭ C D C
sta - tion. Plat - form tick - et, rest - less

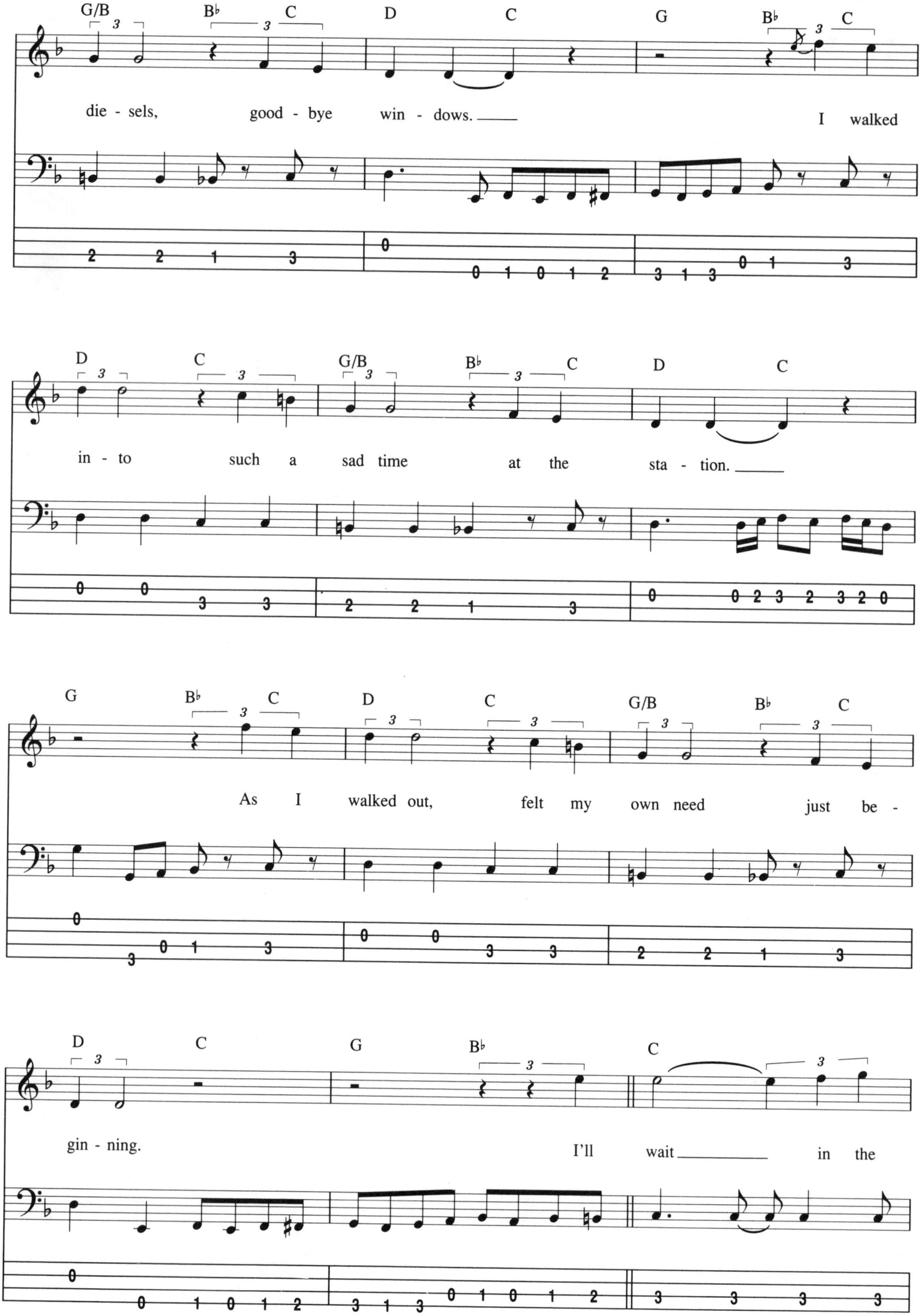
G/B Bb C D C G Bb C
die - sels, good - bye win - dows. I walked
D C G/B Bb C D C
in - to such a sad time at the sta - tion.
G Bb C D C G/B Bb C
As I walked out, felt my own need just be -
D C G Bb C
gin - ning. I'll wait in the

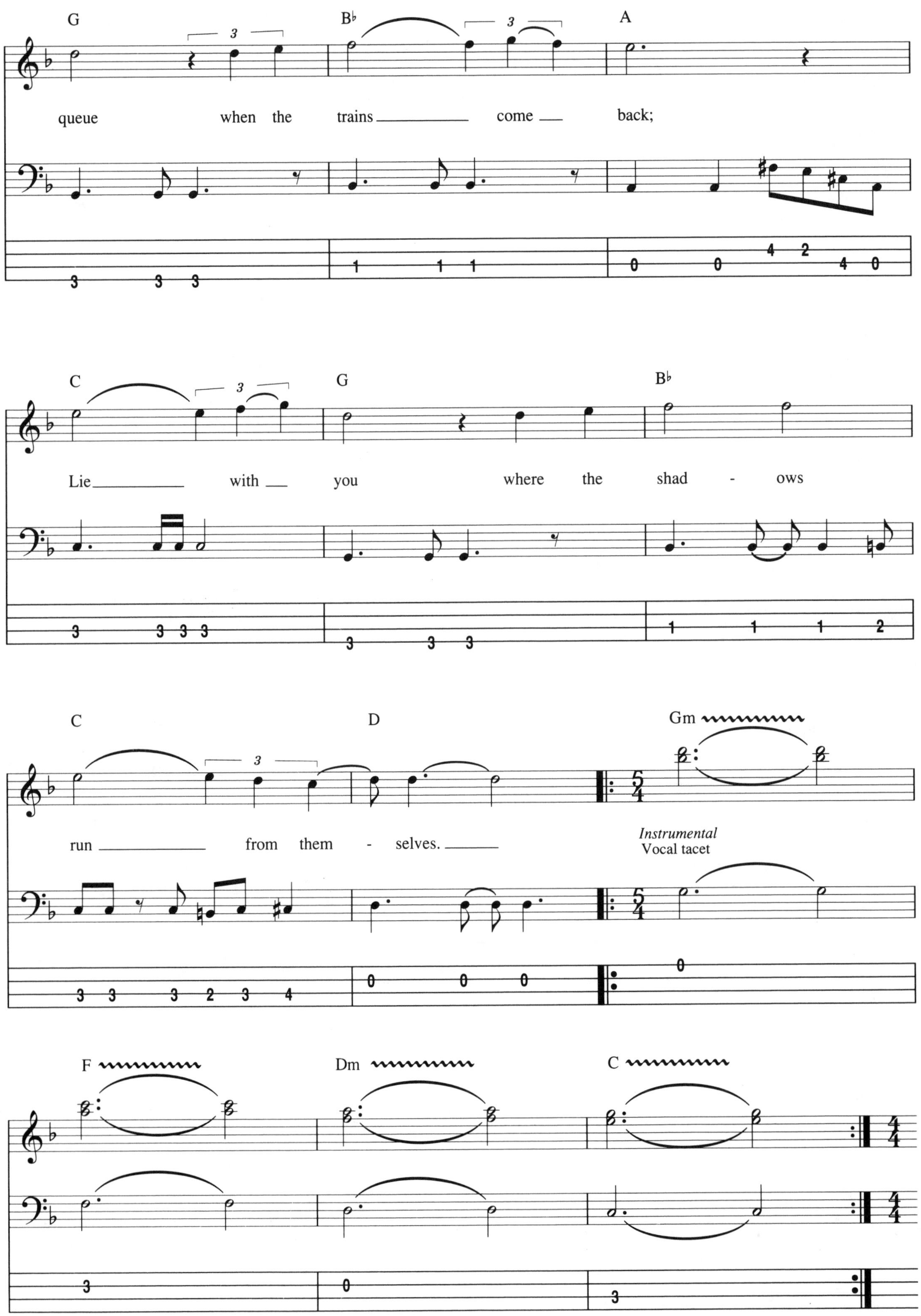
G
B♭
A
queue when the trains come back;
C
G
B♭
Lie with you where the shad - ows
C
D
Gm
run from them - selves.
Instrumental
Vocal tacet
F
Dm
C

Am7
N.C.
D
C
G/B
B♭
C
At the par - ty she was kind - ness in the
D
C
G
B♭
C
D
C
hard crowd. Con - so - la - tion for the
G/B
B♭
C
D
C
G
B♭
C
old wound now for - got - ten. Yel - low
D
C
G/B
B♭
C
D
C
ti - gers crouched in jun - gles in the dark eyes.

G Bb C D C G/B Bb C
She's just dress - ing, good - bye win - dows tired
D C G/B Bb C
star - lings. I'll sleep in this
G Bb A
place with the lone - ly crowd;
C G Bb
lie in the dark where the shad - ows

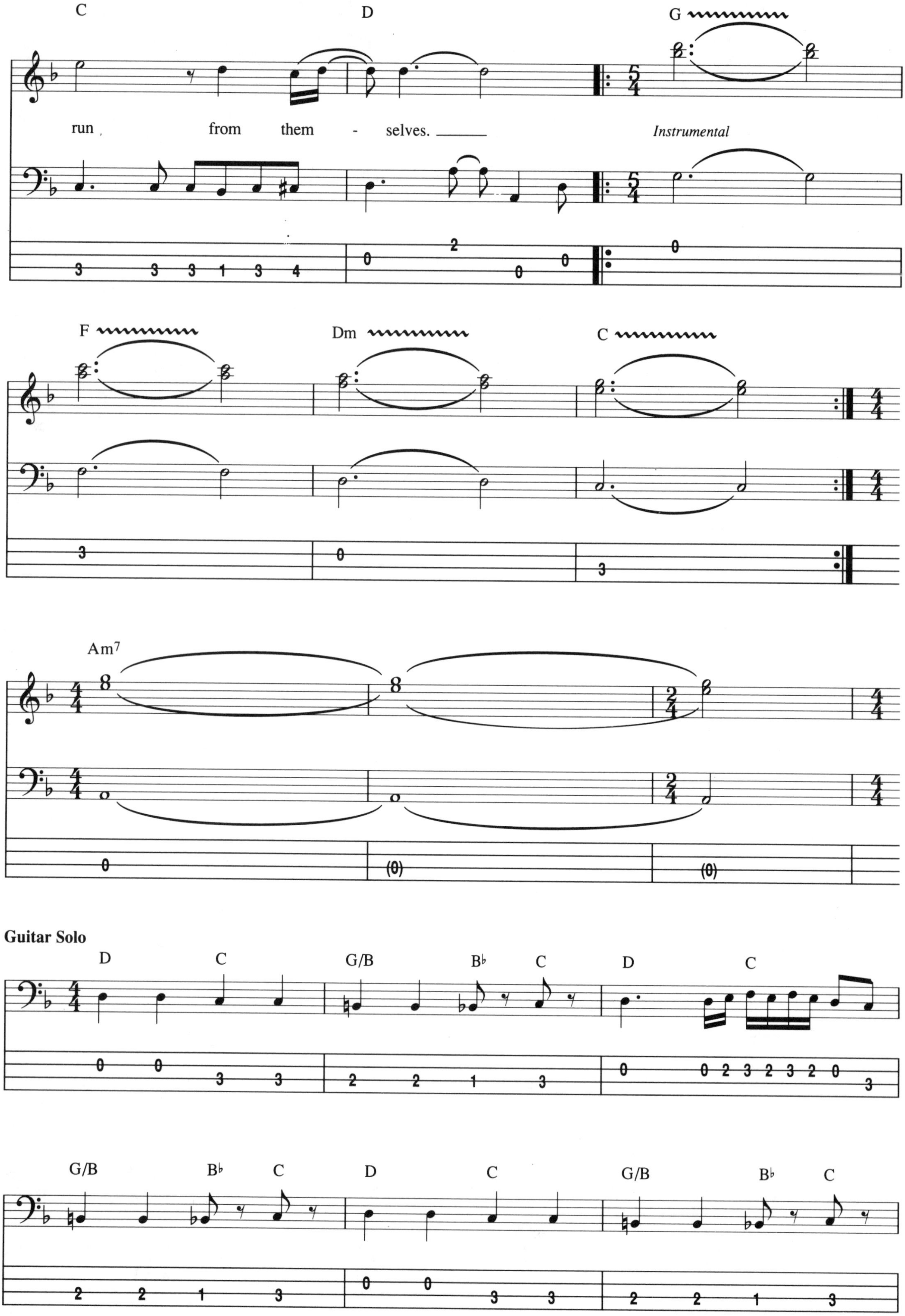
C
D
G
run, from them - selves.
Instrumental
F
Dm
C
Am7
Guitar Solo
D
C
G/B
B♭
C
D
C
G/B
B♭
C
D
C
G/B
B♭
C

D C G/B B♭ C D C G/B B♭ C
D C G/B B♭ C D C G/B B♭ C
D C G B♭ C D C G B♭ C
fade
D C G B♭ C D C G B♭ C
D C G B♭ C D C G B♭ C

You Shook Me

Written by Willie Dixon and J.B. Lenoir

Intro
Slow Blues ♩. = 53
N.C.
A7
E7
mf

Verse
B7
E7
1. You know you shook me, _ you shook me all _ night long. _
2., 3. See additional lyrics

2nd time, w/ Bass Fill 1
A7
You know you shook _ me ba - by, _

Bass Fill 1

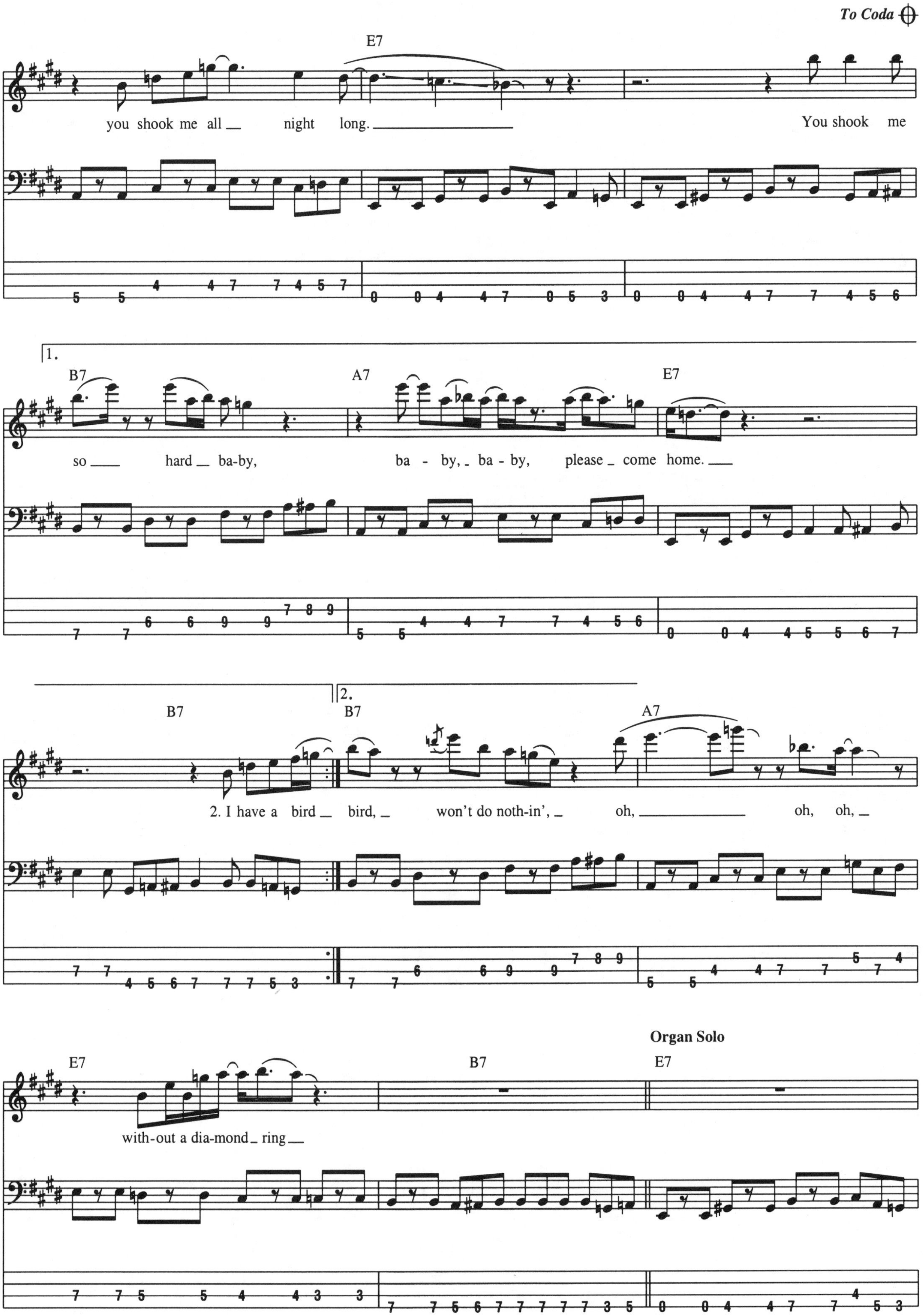

To Coda
E7
you shook me all night long.
You shook me
1.
B7
A7
E7
so hard ba-by,
ba - by, ba - by, please come home.
B7
2.
B7
A7
2. I have a bird bird, won't do noth-in', oh, oh, oh,
Organ Solo
E7
B7
E7
with-out a dia-mond ring

A7
E7
B7
A7
Harmonica Solo
E
Am
A#°
E7/B
B7
E7
A7
E7

B7
A7
E7
Guitar Solo
E7
A5
E7
B7
D.S. al Coda
A7
E7
B7
3
3. You _ know you

Additional Lyrics

2. I have a bird that whistles and
I have birds that sing.
I have a bird that whistles and
I have birds that sing.
I have a bird won't do nothin; oh, oh, oh, oh,
Without a diamond ring.

3. You know you shook me, babe,
You shook me all night long.
I know you really, really did, babe.
I think you shook me, baby,
You shook me all night long.
You shook me so hard, baby, I know.

Bass Notation Legend

Bass music can be notated two different ways: on a *musical staff*, and in *tablature*.

THE MUSICAL STAFF shows pitches and rhythms and is divided by bar lines into measures. Pitches are named after the first seven letters of the alphabet.

TABLATURE graphically represents the bass fingerboard. Each horizontal line represents a string, and each number represents a fret.

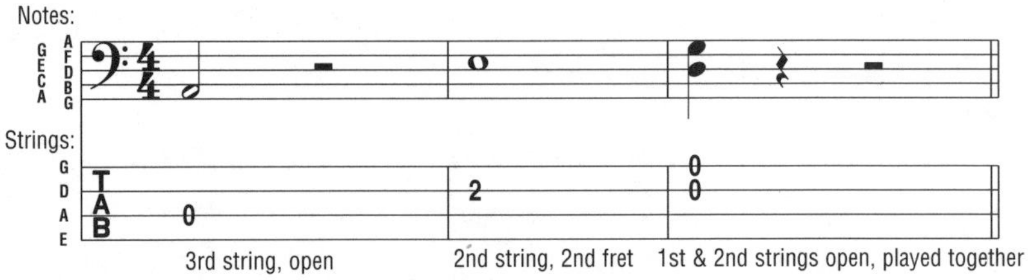

Notes:
Strings:
3rd string, open
2nd string, 2nd fret
1st & 2nd strings open, played together

HAMMER-ON: Strike the first (lower) note with one finger, then sound the higher note (on the same string) with another finger by fretting it without picking.

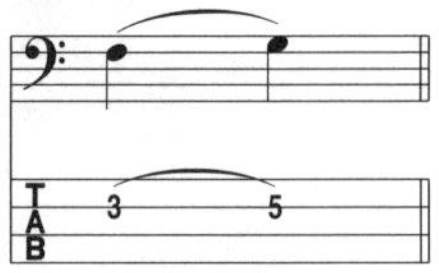

PULL-OFF: Place both fingers on the notes to be sounded. Strike the first note and without picking, pull the finger off to sound the second (lower) note.

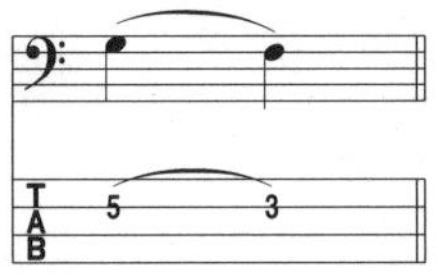

LEGATO SLIDE: Strike the first note and then slide the same fret-hand finger up or down to the second note. The second note is not struck.

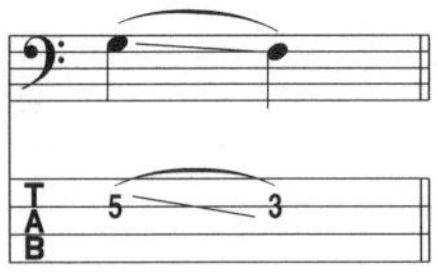

SHIFT SLIDE: Same as legato slide, except the second note is struck.

TRILL: Very rapidly alternate between the notes indicated by continuously hammering on and pulling off.

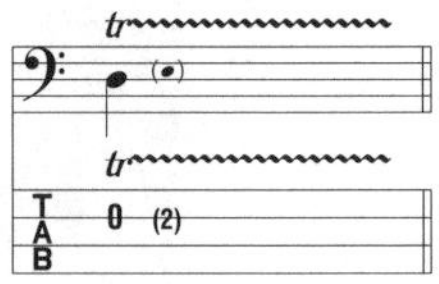

TREMOLO PICKING: The note is picked as rapidly and continuously as possible.

VIBRATO: The string is vibrated by rapidly bending and releasing the note with the fretting hand.

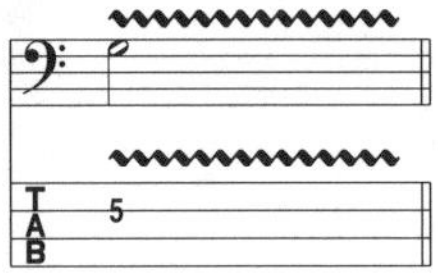

SHAKE: Using one finger, rapidly alternate between two notes on one string by sliding either a half-step above or below.

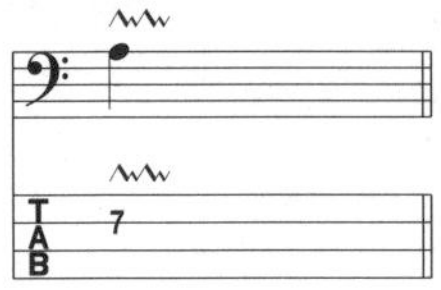

NATURAL HARMONIC: Strike the note while the fret hand lightly touches the string directly over the fret indicated.

Harm.

MUFFLED STRINGS: A percussive sound is produced by laying the fret hand across the string(s) without depressing them and striking them with the pick hand.

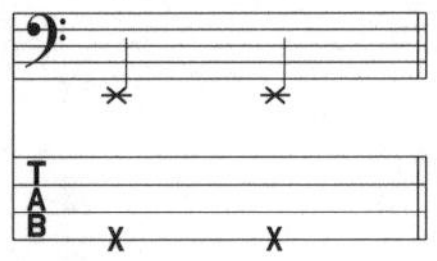

BEND: Strike the note and bend up the interval shown.

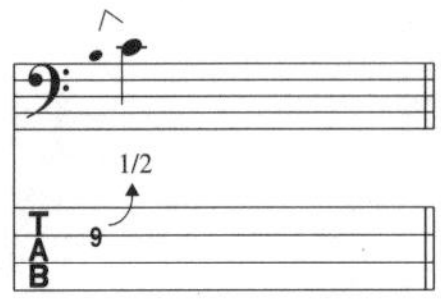

1/2

BEND AND RELEASE: Strike the note and bend up as indicated, then release back to the original note. Only the first note is struck.

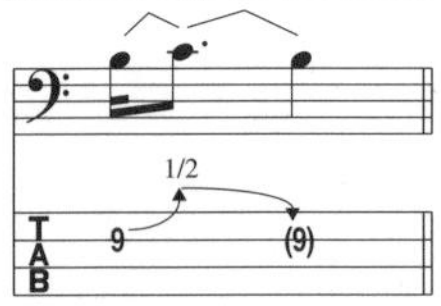

1/2

RIGHT-HAND TAP: Hammer ("tap") the fret indicated with the "pick-hand" index or middle finger and pull off to the note fretted by the fret hand.

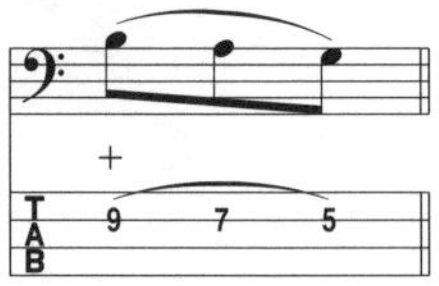

LEFT-HAND TAP: Hammer ("tap") the fret indicated with the "fret-hand" index or middle finger.

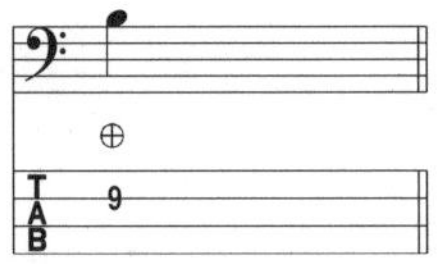

SLAP: Strike ("slap") string with right-hand thumb.

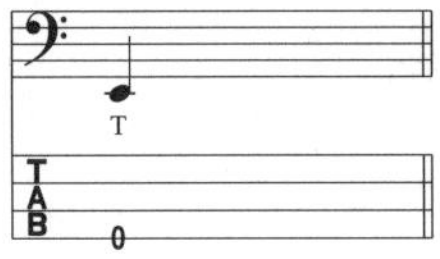

T

POP: Snap ("pop") string with right-hand index or middle finger.

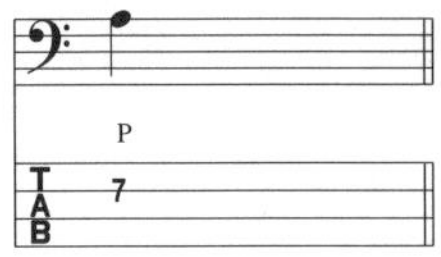

P

Additional Musical Definitions

 *(accent)* • Accentuate note (play it louder)

 *(accent)* • Accentuate note with great intensity

 *(staccato)* • Play the note short

⊓ • Downstroke

V • Upstroke

D.S. al Coda • Go back to the sign (𝄋), then play until the measure marked "***To Coda***," then skip to the section labelled "***Coda***."

D.C. al Fine • Go back to the beginning of the song and play until the measure marked "***Fine***" (end).

Bass Fig. • Label used to recall a recurring pattern.

Fill • Label used to identify a brief pattern which is to be inserted into the arrangement.

tacet • Instrument is silent (drops out).

 • Repeat measures between signs.

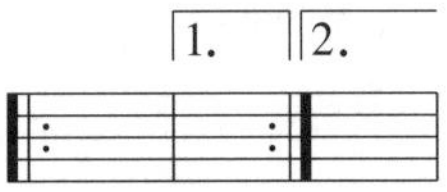

1.
2.

• When a repeated section has different endings, play the first ending only the first time and the second ending only the second time.

NOTE: Tablature numbers in parentheses mean:
1. The note is being sustained over a system (note in standard notation is tied), or
2. The note is sustained, but a new articulation (such as a hammer-on, pull-off, slide or vibrato begins), or
3. The note is a barely audible "ghost" note (note in standard notation is also in parentheses).

BASS RECORDED VERSIONS

Bass Recorded Versions are straight off-the-record transcriptions done expressly for bass guitar. This series features the best in bass licks from the classics to contemporary superstars. Also available are Recorded Versions for Guitar, Easy Recorded Versions and Drum Recorded Versions. Every book includes notes and tab.

Beatles Bass Book
00660103 / $14.95

Best Bass Rock Hits
00694803 / $12.95

Black Sabbath – We Sold Our Soul For Rock 'N' Roll
00660116 / $14.95

The Best of Eric Clapton
00660187 / $14.95

Stuart Hamm Bass Boo[k]
00694823 / $19.95

Jimi Hendrix – Are You Experienced?
00690371 / $14.95

Jimi Hendrix – Axis Bold As Love
00690373 / $14.95

Jimi Hendrix – Electric Ladyland
00690375 / $14.95

The Buddy Holly Bass Book
00660132 / $12.95

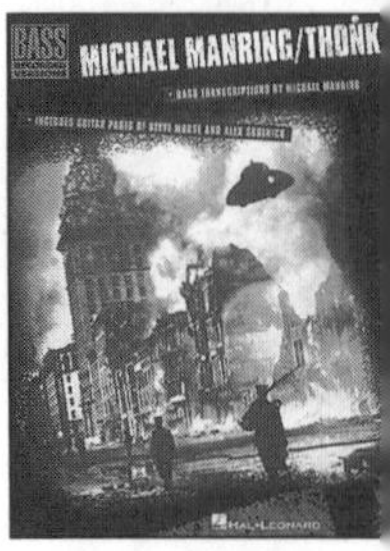

Michael Manring – Thonk
00694924 / $22.95

Motown Bass Classics
00690253 / $14.95

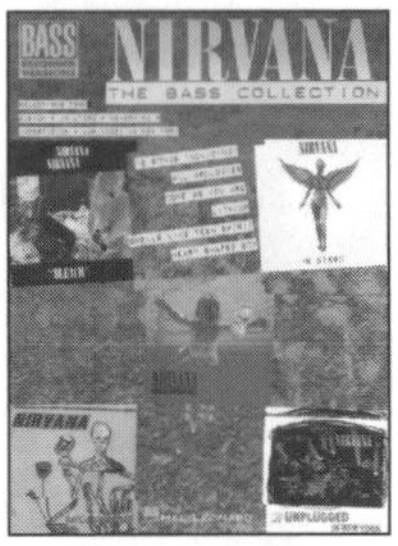

Nirvana Bass Collection
00690066 / $17.95

Pearl Jam – Ten
00694882 / $14.95

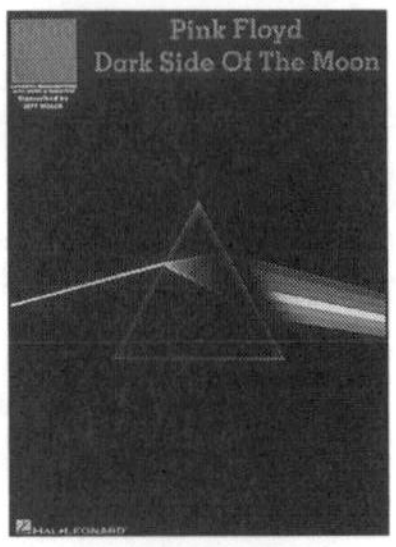

Pink Floyd – Dark Side of the Moon
00660172 / $14.95

The Best of Police
00660207 / $14.95

Queen – The Bass Collection
00690065 / $17.95

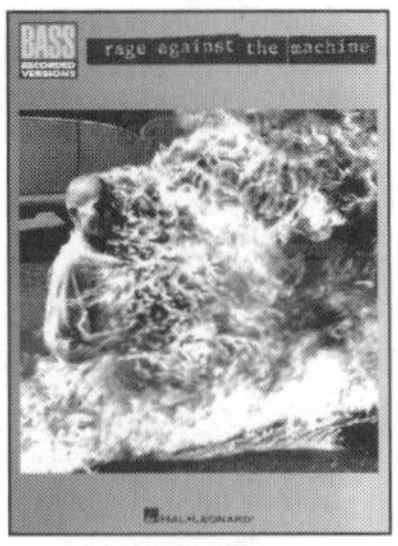

Rage Against the Machine
00690248 / $14.95

Rage Against the Machine – Evil Empire
00690249 / $14.95

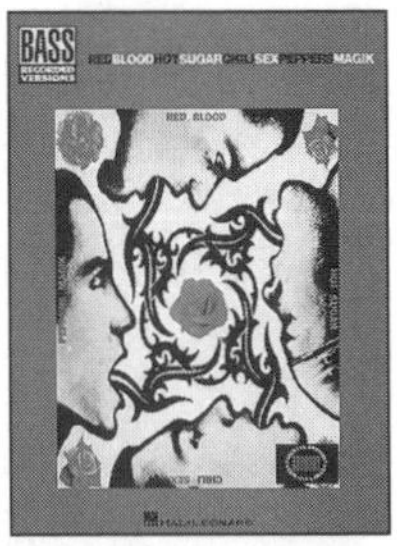

Red Hot Chili Peppers – Blood Sugar Sex Magik
00690064 / $17.95

Red Hot Chili Peppers Californication
00690390 / $19.95

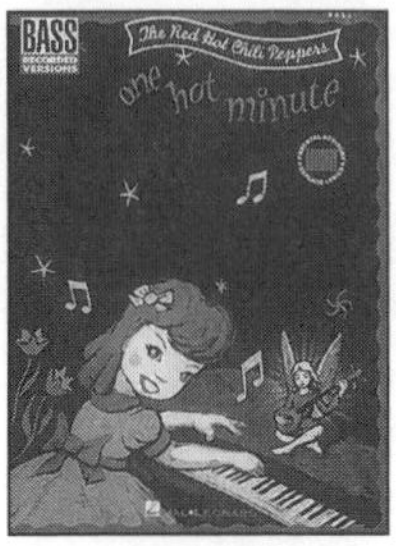

Red Hot Chili Peppers – One Hot Minute
00690091 / $18.95

Rolling Stones
00690256 / $14.95

FOR MORE INFORMATION, SEE YOUR LOCAL MUSIC DEALER, OR WRITE TO:

HAL•LEONARD® CORPORATION
7777 W. BLUEMOUND RD. P.O. BOX 13819 MILWAUKEE, WI 53213

Visit Hal Leonard Online at
www.halleonard.com

Prices, contents & availability subject to change without notice. Some products may not be available outside the U.S.A.

Stevie Ray Vaughan – In Step
00694777 / $14.95

Stevie Ray Vaughan Lightnin' Blues 1983-1[987]
00694778 / $19.95

02